Joining the WTO

T0316972

European University Studies

Europäische Hochschulschriften
Publications Universitaires Européennes

Series XXXI
Political Science

Reihe XXXI   Série XXXI
Politikwissenschaft
Sciences politiques

Vol./Bd. 550

PETER LANG

Frankfurt am Main · Berlin · Bern · Bruxelles · New York · Oxford · Wien

Christian Kraft

Joining the WTO

The Impact of Trade, Competition and Redistributive Conflicts on China's Accession to the World Trade Organization

PETER LANG
Internationaler Verlag der Wissenschaften

Bibliographic Information published by the Deutsche Nationalbibliothek
The Deutsche Nationalbibliothek lists this publication in the Deutsche Nationalbibliografie; detailed bibliographic data is available in the internet at <http://www.d-nb.de>.

Zugl.: Konstanz, Univ., Diss., 2006

D 352
ISSN 0721-3654
ISBN 978-3-631-56773-9

© Peter Lang GmbH
Internationaler Verlag der Wissenschaften
Frankfurt am Main 2007
All rights reserved.

Printed in Germany 1 2 3 4 5   7

www.peterlang.de

TABLE OF CONTENTS

ACKNOWLEDGEMENTS

A large number of people supported me directly or indirectly during the conceptualization and the writing of this book. My colleagues at the University of Konstanz, friends and family were always present with motivating words and constructive criticism at any stage of the project – many thanks to all of them.

PD Dr. Thomas Plümper, my supervisor at the University of Konstanz, initiated the DFG-Project "The Political Economy of Conditional and Discriminatory Membership in International Institutions" and thereby created the framework for this book. I especially thank Thomas Plümper for his support and for giving me the opportunity to participate in the research project. Special thanks also go to Professor Dr. Gerald Schneider for endorsing me over the past years and for his interest in evaluating this work as a second referee.

I thank my colleague Christina Schneider for the frequent, manifold and fruitful discussions, which accelerated the progress of this project. I also thank the initiators and the participants of the doctoral seminars at the Department of Politics and Management for their helpful comments and the German Research Foundation (DFG) for financing the project.

Last but not least, I am grateful to my parents and to my wife Vera for always supporting me.

Konstanz, May 2007
Christian Kraft

LIST OF FIGURES

LIST OF TABLES

1 INTRODUCTION

The World Trade Organization's (WTO) primary objective is to promote trade between its 149 current members. Ironically, the world's fastest growing trading nation – the People's Republic of China (PRC) – was excluded from the organization until December of 2001. In 1998, twelve years past its application for membership and three years before China finally joined the WTO, Long Yongtu, chief Chinese accession negotiator and at that time deputy minister of the Ministry of Foreign Trade and Economic Cooperation, gave a speech at the Central Party School dealing with the current status of WTO accession negotiations and justifying China's membership ambitions.

Besides highlighting expected benefits from China's prospective WTO membership, he also clarified that "… joining the WTO does not mean that we are opening up our markets across the board; instead, all it means is that we will open up our markets conditionally. These conditions will result from negotiations that are being discussed and bargained for by our negotiating team or delegation in talks with the delegates of other countries, under the direct leadership of our Central Government and our Party's Central Committee. And if our joining the WTO would mean a major adverse impact on our industries, then we would rather not join the WTO" (Long Yongtu 2000: 51). And in fact, from this day on China has not joined the WTO for another three years.

Asking why negotiations dragged on for so long without reaching decisions, Long Yongtu contends that the primary reason "… is that these negotiations happened to take place precisely during a period of time in which our country's economy – and especially our country's foreign trade – was growing at high speed." As a consequence of this economic growth, the WTO adopted "… what can be called an attitude of applying higher standards and more demanding criteria" (Long Yongtu 2000: 6).

But since the WTO is a member driven organization, it was not the WTO as an institution which demanded higher standards and more demanding criteria, but *individual member governments,* who negotiated future trade relations and the timing of accession with Chinese delegates. In these negotiations, central to the WTO accession process, deadlock occurs when sceptical governments oppose China's accession for exactly the same reasons as Long Yongtu's considerations not to join in the first place: they are unwilling to accept China as a new WTO member because its accelerated growth coupled with substantial liberalization of foreign trade would exert an adverse redistributive impact on their own industries, that is, increased competition for a multitude of labour intense manufactures at home and abroad on world markets. Increasing competition from WTO enlargement triggers domestic income redistribution as commonly modelled by the political economy of trade and protection. The core argument is thus, that redistributive effects directly cause conflicts in WTO enlargement negotiations and increase protectionist measures towards countries applying for WTO membership.

1.1 The Logic of Redistributive Conflicts

Redistributive conflicts in WTO enlargement negotiations emerge on at least three levels. First, the influx of cheap goods from candidate countries to old WTO members threatens domestic import-competing industries. Governments trying to protect those uncompetitive but domestically powerful industries potentially oppose WTO enlargement and demand ongoing trade restrictions for the candidate in the case of accession. This first line of conflict hence pits candidates against protectionist WTO members. The utilization of WTO antidumping regulations for protectionist purposes partly solves this conflict. This form of 'contingent protection' enables governments to further protect powerful industries past enlargement.

Second and moreover, if WTO accession enables candidates to strengthen their comparative advantages in special export sectors, the stress of competition rises for identical sectors of old members on international markets. Thus, candidates challenge the status quo of established exporters on world markets. This situation, dubbed 'third-market competition', triggers a redistributive conflict among export sectors of similarly endowed old members and applicant countries. Third-market competition originates abroad as a consequence of other countries' trade relations. Governments confronted with large export industries facing negative welfare effects from increasing competition by the new member are powerless to counteract. The only solution to prolong quota rents for domestic exporters on hard-fought world markets is to delay the candidate's accession process.

Third, close trading partners of the applicant countries profit from better market access and will therefore favour their membership. The pro-integration attitude of members exporting to a respective candidate finally triggers conflicts with those members opposing accession for protectionist motives.

The theoretical arguments within this book are illustrated and empirically tested with China's accession to the WTO. China constitutes a crucial case among all WTO accession since 1995. Due to its WTO outsider status despite its accelerated economic growth throughout the 1990s China is suited best to analyze the influence of redistributive conflicts from trade liberalization on problems occurring during enlargement negotiations of multilateral trade agreements.

Surprisingly, the voluminous literature on WTO enlargement in general and China's accession to the WTO in particular neglect redistributive income effects, the consequential conflicts in negotiations, accession delay and discriminatory membership rights. Since its foundation in 1995, the lion's share of new members consists of newly industrialized and transition economies. Explaining stumbling blocs to these countries' WTO accessions, previous research exclusively focuses on the difficulties of bringing the respective countries' trade policies in line with WTO rules.

Thus, WTO accession literature is mostly concerned with systemic explanations, attributing lengthy accession procedures to home-made deficiencies and reform reluctance of the applicants themselves: The slow pace of reforming centrally planned to market oriented economies, the persistence of state owned enterprises, ongoing subsidization, lacking protection of intellectual property rights and infant industry protection of newly emerging service sectors are the most prominent obstacles to free-trade in transition-, developing- and newly industrialized economies (Yang 1999).

In contrast, this analysis focuses on other members' preferences on WTO enlargement, depending on their economic gains and losses from negotiated trade liberalization measures with the candidate. Home-made trade policy deficiencies of applicant countries can hence not fully explain the time consuming enlargement negotiations if old members general oppose their accession on the basis of protectionist motives.

The political economy of trade and protection offers the basis for further theoretical considerations within this book. Sound theoretical models generate clear cut predictions for income redistributions from losers to winners of bilateral trade liberalization between two countries (Milner 1988; Krugman 1991; Hillman 2003). Trade liberalization at the core of the WTO enlargement process is however multilateral in effect. The models are therefore extended to the multilateral WTO accession scenario. Under the assumption that an economic important country seeks entry to the WTO, the theory predicts that declining import-competitors and exporters facing increased competition on foreign markets generally oppose enlargement, while exporters capable of extending sales to the applicant favour its accession.

A number of empirical approaches confirm such redistributive effects for the crucial cases of China's WTO accession. China's accelerated economic growth, coupled with its prospective WTO membership significantly increases the competition stress for other WTO countries and industries. Besides declining import-competing industries in industrial countries, similarly endowed developing countries have difficulties in competing with Chinese producers of labour intensive manufactures on international markets (Ianchovichina and Walmsley 2005; Shafaeddin 2002; Sussangkarn 2004). China's WTO accession hence plays an important role for increasing international competition: it brings Chinese exporters equal access to foreign markets and eliminates other members' quota rents (Anderson 1997). In other words, a negative effect of China's WTO accession on other members' economies has been empirically proven in many cases, but has not been considered as a source for conflict in WTO enlargement negotiations.

Subsequent to the theorization of redistributive effects, the two separate but complementary theories within this book explain how governments of adversely affected import-competing and export-competing industries utilize accession negotiations to counteract income losses from WTO enlargement. First, governments constrained by powerful import-competing industries increase the number of antidumping measures to offer ongoing protection in the case of new members' accession (Chapter 4). Second, since governments are powerless to protect exporters from increasing third-market competition, they impede accession negotiations and delay candidates' membership (Chapter 5). Thus, theoretical considerations complement the WTO accession literature by a further stumbling bloc to unconditional enlargement: old members' strategic opposition and protection due to the fear of increasing competition for domestic industries.

1.2 The Impact on China's Accession to the WTO

The empirical section of Chapter 4 is dedicated to the test of protectionist responses to China's WTO accession motivated by the fear of increasing import-competition. It demonstrates that China has become the world's major anti-dumping target throughout the late 1990s prior to its WTO accession in 2001. Panel regression results largely confirm the expectation that countries with import-competing industries negatively affected by China increase the level of contingent protection with the increasing probability of China entering the WTO. More specifically, industry-specific AD measures against China are found to be a function of the import penetration ratio, the respective industry's size, its labour intensity and its fear of Chinese retaliation. These effects grow stronger over time towards China's WTO membership and thereafter. Overall, the results support the argument that members replace traditional trade barriers against China by subtle AD duties, thereby reducing domestic opposition against WTO trade liberalization accompanied by enlargement.

Second, China's accelerated growth in especially labour intensive manufactures and its consequential export power also challenges old members' exporters worldwide. WTO membership grants Chinese exporters equal access to economies of established members and thus increase the competitive pressure for old members' exporters. In Chapter 5, a case study sketches the logic of third third-market competition as a source of strategic delay in China's accession negotiations.

The results are mixed and confirm both traditional explanations for China's long way to the WTO, that is, reform reluctance and political incidences *and* the logic of individual members delaying accession. Moreover, the case study demonstrates China's 15 year long and cumbersome accession negotiations. In the first phase, incidences such as the Beijing Massacre at Tiananmen Square in 1989 hampered China's accession ambitions due to the loss of international credibility. Throughout the 1990s up to today, China has also been much criticized for the insufficient reduction of state owned enterprises, ongoing subsidization, lacking liberalization of service sectors and finally for not protecting intellectual property rights. Speeding up these matters would doubtlessly have accelerated China's membership.

However, the case study also uncovers intended delay by individual members, who display – as theoretically predicted – similar export structures relative to

China in especially technical manufactures exhibiting exorbitant growth rates in China. Especially Mexico, India, Malaysia, Thailand and Poland have been last minute negotiators, who – by retarding individual bilateral agreements – also delayed the date of accession. The most crucial case is Mexico, which was reluctant to reach an agreement with Chinese delegates even one year after all critical issues with other members – including the European Union (EU) and the USA – had been solved.

The joined results confirm the bottom line argument that individual members, trying to protect domestic industries from redistributive income effects, opposed China's accession. Those governments exclusively pressured by import-competitors can solve the dilemma with contingent protection; those facing opposition from adversely affected exporters on third-markets are inclined to delay accession to prolong quota rents. Either way derogates China's gains from free-trade and hence its major benefit from WTO membership. Since 2001, China has finally enjoyed equal membership rights, although its trade is still restricted by antidumping and safeguard measures.

Chapter 6 traces China's utilization of its WTO membership since 2001 and asks if Chinese officials utilize the newly gained membership rights to retaliate against those members, who opposed its accession in the first place. It is shown that China's own antidumping activities indeed skyrocketed in 2002 – immediately after its WTO accession. While these measures are exclusively directed at other antidumping users in a club-like manner, the Chinese government abstains from punishing those who have been most protectionist during its accession procedure. A similar pattern arises for China's participation in the WTO dispute settlement procedure. Its indirect dispute involvement as a third-party increased sharply past accession, but Chinese officials only complained once directly against unfair trade practices of the USA. Hence, China increasingly utilizes its newly gained WTO membership rights to strengthen its trade relations rather than triggering trade disputes or retaliating against other members

1.3 Implications for WTO Accession Research

All in all, by theorizing the emergence of redistributive conflicts from WTO enlargement and the consequences for interstate conflicts in WTO accession negotiations, and by testing and illustrating the mechanisms by means of quantitative and qualitative methods, this work contributes to the understanding of WTO accessions and free-trade enlargement in four different ways.

First and in general terms, it complements WTO and free-trade enlargement research with an analytical account of other members' role in the accession game. So far, the slow pace of negotiations and suboptimal outcomes – from new members' point of view – was mainly attributed to applicants themselves. This book shows that home-made reform deficiencies are not sufficient to explain accession delay and limited membership rights if old members have reasons to oppose the respective applicant's accession as a function of the redistributive conflicts of its economic integration. Instead, opponents can use slow pace of reform as a lame excuse for not enlarging the trade club.

Second, this analysis complements theories of multilateral trade liberalization by contending that exporters potentially lose from emerging third-market competition. Models based on specific-factor assumptions commonly model exporters as the winners of bilateral and reciprocal trade liberalization. However, when two or more bilateral trade agreements turn multilateral in effect – as in the case of WTO enlargement – the bilaterally reached agreements interact. Competition for exporters of a given country potentially increases as a function of tariff reductions negotiated by other countries. Considering that 149 WTO members negotiate trade liberalization for thousands of different goods and services, third-market effects are extensive, which seriously hampers multilateral trade ambitions. Exporters suffering from the multilateral integration of powerful new members such as China hence need to be incorporated into the accession literature as a strong source for negotiation conflicts. Moreover, liberalization theories generally treating export oriented industries as free-traders should take account of potential income losses for exporters when liberalization is multilateral.

Third, the logic of third-market competition contributes to the understanding of problems emerging in future WTO enlargement. The main line of argument in previous research contends that especially high-income nations hamper the accession process of new WTO members to protect import-competitors from the influx of cheap goods. However, equally endowed countries – compared to the applicant – are the ones affected by third-market competition. Remaining WTO outsiders, all of which are either developing, newly industrialized or transition economies, will face additional opposition by equally structured, potentially neighbouring countries. In other words, significant third-market competition adds a South-South divide to the traditional North-South cleavage of WTO trade liberalization.

Fourth and finally, the analysis of AD measures filed against China during its accession period and filed by China thereafter contributes to the empirical research on contingent protection. Rather than focussing on one industrial country as an AD user, this book quantitatively analyses the motives of WTO member countries and industries to apply antidumping against one newly industrialized target country. This change of perspective compared to previous research shows that the impact factors of antidumping against China – e.g. the import penetration ratio, industry size and the fear of future Chinese retaliation – are relatively homogenous for a heterogeneous set of countries.

1.4 Structure of the Book

The book is organized as follows. Chapter 2 first reviews previous research done in the field of the political economy of trade and protection. These theoretical approaches enable the detection of redistributive effects from free-trade, and thus from WTO enlargement. Focussing on bilateral relations, this literature offers sound predictions for import-competitors being the losers of trade liberalization, but misses out on third-market competition, which has empirically been identified for the crucial case of China's WTO accession by case specific economic approaches. Research on antidumping and contingent protection is finally surveyed to lay the foundation for modelling protectionist responses to WTO enlargement.

Chapter 3 offers background information on WTO membership benefits, the accession process, the formation of the working party (WP) and explains the choice and the key characteristics of China as a crucial case for upcoming analyses. It especially illuminates the central proceeding of bilateral market access negotiations, describes the WP members as the sample countries and offers a technical description of how the WTO rules of accession supply these countries with sufficient leverage to delay individual bilateral negotiations.

Chapter 4 elaborates the first line of conflicts in China's accession negotiations and their solution. Its theoretical section contends that member governments react with contingent protection to China's membership ambitions, which is largely confirmed by the quantitative analysis of members' antidumping practices against Chinese goods. Subsequent to these findings, Chapter 5 argues that governments are comparably powerless if China challenges exporters on third-markets. Delaying accession negotiations is the only way of prolonging quota rents for old members' export oriented industries. The case study of Chapter 5 displays that a number of newly industrialized countries competing with China on world markets have in fact been reluctant negotiators in the 15 year long accession process.

Chapter 6 tops off the analysis by tracing China's evolution as a new WTO member since 2002, while focusing on the question whether the Chinese government tends to retaliate upon those members who opposed its accession in the first place. The comparison of China's antidumping and trade disputes practices with those of old members uncover that China is evolving into a rather cooperative new member to the WTO. Finally, Chapter 7 summarizes the results, puts them into a broader perspective and searches for analogies to current WTO applicants.

2 WTO Enlargement: Previous Research

Literature on WTO enlargement is voluminous but deals mainly with general WTO accession "Issues and Challenges" (Yang 1999: 513), being concerned with the factors impacting candidates' time consuming accession processes. The mostly descriptive narratives commonly define applicants' incapability of bringing their domestic economic system in line with WTO rules, which "...involves not only liberalization of economic activities, but also fundamental changes in the rules of the game and the social and economic institutions." (Yang 1999: 518).

The list of obstacles to domestic reform and hence to WTO membership is long, but emerges exclusively from the fact that the majority of new WTO members and current applicants are countries in transition with previously centrally planned economies. In contrast, WTO membership conditions prescribe market oriented systems. Hence, this literature attributes the slow accession process mainly to factors such as the persistence of large state sectors, which have so far been protected from competition, infant industry protection to newly emerging service sectors, ongoing non-tariff barriers to trade or lacking protection of intellectual property rights (Broude 1998; Langhammer and Lücke 1999; Michalopoulos 1998; Panitchpakdi and Clifford 2002; van der Geest 1998; Wei 1998; Yang 1999).

This literature neglects however a closer analysis of the core proceeding inherent to all WTO accessions: the multilateral trade liberalization between the candidate and WTO members. The trade agreements reached after numerous bargaining rounds trigger far reaching redistributive income effects as analyzed by the political economy of trade and protection. Nevertheless, previous research explaining obstacles to individual WTO accessions ignore the conflicts arising from multilateral tariff reductions necessary for accepting new members to the WTO.

To close this gap, this analysis draws on theories of international trade and protection to model domestic redistributive income conflicts from WTO enlargement as determinants for member governments' attitudes towards WTO candidate countries. The next section thus surveys approaches capable to explain the effects of trade liberalization on domestic industries. Unfortunately, this literature is limited to bilateral and reciprocal trade relations, wherefore it misses out on negative welfare effects for exporters arising in a multilateral setting such as the WTO enlargement procedure. The redistributive effects outlined by this research and the research desideratum of third-market competition are thereafter empirically exemplified with approaches analyzing the economic impact of China's WTO accession on other members. Subsequently, the logic of contingent protection is introduced, which describes the utilization of WTO antidumping regulation as governments' response to increasing import-competition. So far, the analysis of contingent protection is limited to individual users of antidumping measures, but the inherent logic is also applicable to protectionist responses to new WTO members. The last section finally summarizes the previous research, the desideratum and the implications for this work's research questions.

2.1 Redistributive Effects of WTO Enlargement

The primary objective of the WTO is to promote the trade relations among its members. Consequential, the reduction of trade barriers is not only the most controversial and time consuming process during numerous WTO liberalization rounds among its members. Liberalization negotiations also take the centre stage of the WTO accession process. Stated simple, countries applying for WTO membership need to reduce domestic tariff and non-tariff barriers and receive, in return, improved access to other WTO markets. To integrate important countries into the world trade system hence inevitably requires a step towards free trade for the applicant as well as for its trading partners. Seeking to identify the income redistribution from losers to winners of such a step towards freer trade, scholars following the specific-factor approach in the school of political economy of international trade offer a simple solution: export-oriented industries – and factors of production attached to it – gain from new markets abroad and import-competing industries lose from the increasing competition due to domestic tariff reductions (Milner 1988; Krugman 1991; Hillman 2003).[1] The trade policy interests of export-oriented and import-competing industries are thus diametrically opposed in the case of trade liberalization and WTO enlargement (Alt and Gilligan 1994).

---

[1] For further survey see also Milner (1999) or Rodrik (1995)

The exchange of market access is commonly theorized to be reciprocal (Yarbrough and Yarbrough 1986; Bagwell and Staiger 1996, 1997; Rhodes 1989). Governments exchange domestic tariff reductions for market access abroad and maximize political support if marginal gains for exporters exceed marginal losses for import-competitors (Hillman 1989; Hillman and Moser 1996; Finger et al. 2002).

Asking why protectionism persists after bilateral and reciprocal liberalization negotiations have been concluded, scholars commonly blame politically influential import-competitors. According to Hillman (2003: 3) "How much protection each government retains after providing and receiving market access for exporters depends on the relative political influence, or political importance, of export and import-competing industries. The politically optimal exchange of market access need not therefore result in an agreement to eliminate all trade barriers to implement free trade. Reciprocal liberalization will in particular be gradual, if governments are constrained in the magnitude of the income losses that can be imposed at any point in time on the import-competing industries that lose from the reciprocal liberalization."

Theories on international trade and protection thus offer clear-cut predictions about income redistribution from losers to winners in bilateral liberalization scenarios. However, liberalization negotiations in the WTO accession process are multilateral in effect: negotiated tariff reductions between candidate and *one* member apply to the universe of *all* other WTO members once the candidate is accepted.

While liberalization theories based on reciprocity thus perfectly predict trade policy conflicts in bilateral scenarios, they do not account for the externalities caused by their multilateralization. To determine the overall utility of multilateral enlargement, negotiating governments must constantly assess the impact of agreements bilaterally reached by other governments. Ethier (2004: 314) contends that reciprocal liberalization is not implementable due to 'political externalities', which arise "...when policymakers in one country believe that their political status (...) is directly sensitive, to some degree, to actions by policymakers in another country" (Ethier 2004: 305). What Ethier vaguely defines as 'externality' is what theories focussed on bilateral liberalization does not account for: the impact of one negotiation dyad on the gains from other governments' bilateral agreements.

In Chapter 5, I argue that such an externality causes increasing competition for export-oriented corporations of member countries, as other members liberalize their previously protected market for similar exporters of the candidate applying for WTO membership. Competing reciprocal agreements cause a fractionalization of exporters: some win from directly negotiated liberalization, others lose from other states' agreements. Governments constantly assess domestic political support effects on the basis of potential competing reciprocal liberalization agreements.

The crucial case of China's accession to the WTO demonstrates the redistributive effect of negotiating trade liberalization with an important country in the course of WTO enlargement. What appears is, that not only import-competitors oppose tariff reductions for cheap Chinese goods, but that also exporters of similar endowed transition countries face increasing competition on world markets. Consequentially, the upcoming research is a valuable source in the search of motives behind old governments' opposition against China's WTO membership. It fully reveals the economic impact of China's integration on individual member economies. State simply, the identification of winners and losers from China's WTO membership is the best predictor for cleavages in accession negotiations.

2.2 Redistributive Effects of China's Accession to the WTO

Due to China's economic importance coupled with trade liberalization measures along its WTO accession negotiations exemplifies is the best example how WTO enlargement triggers redistributive conflicts among import-competitors, losing and winning exporters. Opponents to and proponents of WTO accession can be best explained by the competitive threats China causes to the respective economies. China's strength lies in the production of labour-intensive manufactures with a special weight on textiles and clothing industries, although Chinese textiles export are still subject to restrictions in the form of transitional safeguard measures (Mallon and Whalley 2004; Rumbaugh and Blancher 2004; Walmsley and Hertel 2000; Wang 2000; Yang 1999). And although "...textiles and clothing are the products of greatest concern..." (Anderson 1997: 765), China's comparative advantage slowly shifts towards more capital-intensive products such as consumer electronics (Ianchovichina and Walmsley 2005).

Due to China's economic power in labour-intense manufactures, scholars mostly agree that similarly endowed developing countries will have difficulties in competing with Chinese producers on international markets (Ianchovichina and Walmsley 2005; Shafaeddin 2002; Sussangkarn 2004). This is not only because of China's rapid growth in exports, but also due to the fact that other developing countries will lose their quota rents with China receiving equal access to their target markets (Anderson 1997).

In contrast, high-income countries and newly industrialized ASEAN countries are generally identified as the overall winners of China's economic integration. Nevertheless, declining import-competing industries within these countries will also suffer heavy losses. Since these 'special interests' (Grossman and Helpman 2001) are famous for their political power, it seems realistic that governments of industrial countries will also pay attention to domestic import-competitors when negotiating China's WTO accession.

In sum, developing countries can be expected to suffer from export-competition, while industrial countries generally profit, but face opposition from domestic import-competitors, or as Anderson (1997: 765) puts it: "The least-competitive firms and workers in both sets of countries are unhappy about that prospect. Hence it is understandable that they oppose their government's efforts to get China into the WTO, arguing that China is an 'unfair' competitor because its state-owned enterprises are often subsidised."

The economic impact on other WTO members – developing or developed – as reflected in this research does not come as a surprise. It is however all the more surprising that this predicted impact has only rarely been theorized, especially with respect to the emerging export competition for developing countries.

Chapter 5 shows that especially the previously underexposed effect of third-market competition bears important implications for the WTO accession process. Equivalent to conflicts arising from increasing import-competition, countries with industries significantly affected by Chinese export-competition will also be more reluctant to China's WTO integration. Since third-competition emerges abroad as a function of other countries trade relations, governments have no tools at hand to protect exporters. If increasing competition is caused by China acceding to the WTO, the only solution for protecting adversely affected export industries is to oppose its membership.

This represents an important source of conflict in accession negotiations. It is thus highly probable that members severely affected by third-market competition delayed China's membership. Nevertheless, among the large amount of scholarly pieces trying to explain stumbling blocs to China's WTO accession, only two – to my knowledge – incidentally mention how export competition affects old members' motives to demand trade distorting measures in bilateral negotiations, thereby delaying the accession process (Gertler 2003; Panitchpakdi and Clifford 2002).

When multilateral trade liberalization increases third-market competition among WTO members, governments are relatively powerless to counteract – that is to protect exporters exposed to income losses. When third-market competition emerges from the accession of new members, the simplest way to reduce negative welfare effects for exporters is to oppose the accession process, as will be argued in Chapter 5.

In contrast, the following section surveys approaches explaining WTO members' reaction to increasing import-competition. This literature on 'contingent protection' (Tharakan 1995) describes the utilization of antidumping protection to limit negative welfare effects for import-competitors from trade liberalization. As such, 'contingent protection' is also suitable to limit redistributive effects arising from WTO enlargement and can hence decrease import-competitors' opposition to accepting new WTO members, as analyzed in Chapter 4.

2.3 Antidumping and Contingent Protection

A prominent tool for legally limiting imports to domestic markets among WTO members is the filing of antidumping measures. Simple spoken, antidumping measures in the form of import quotas or tariffs are justified if imports are sold at lower prices on the target market than in the exporting country (WTO 1994: Article 2.1). The filing of AD measures has been dubbed 'contingent protection' in the political economy literature on trade and protection (Blonigen and Prusa 2001; Feaver and Wilson 2004; Messerlin and Tharakan 1999; Tharakan 1995).

The core argument of this research is that the loopholes, the vague nature and the lack of transparency of the AD procedure enable national governments and authorities to utilize AD measures for the focused protection of domestic special interests. As Messerlin and Tharakan (1999: 1258) put it "... the empirical studies which analyse the operation of the antidumping system find that the AD system is basically a flexible tool for preventing imports, whether dumped or not, from causing injury to domestic industry." Comprehensive empirical approaches mostly focus on industrial countries as users of contingent protection.

Banks (1993) as well as Feaver and Wilson (2004) offer a comprehensive explanation of the main impact factors on protectionist bias in Australian antidumping decision-making. Besides the traditional political economy explanations of political supply-side and industrial demand-side pressures for protectionist policies, they also identify unintended protectionist bias in the regulatory process. Feaver's and Wilson's (2004) empirical findings support this regulatory bias for Australian AD filings: Industries applying for AD benefit from regulatory deficiencies in the Australian system.

Others deal with protectionist tendencies in the administration of US AD filings, of which only a small fraction has been a reaction to truly uncompetitive behaviour of foreign firms (Baldwin 1998; Hyun Ja Shin 1998). Canadian authorities have also proven to be generous in providing remedies to industries which complained to be negatively affected by foreign dumping practices (Dutz 1998).

The EU constitutes a special case with respect to AD administration, which is subject to the European Commission. AD filings should hence be less sensitive to national protectionist demands. But despite this formal autonomy, Bourgeois and Messerlin (1998) point out that a simple majority in the European Council is also sufficient for a positive antidumping decision. Furthermore, if the Commission plans on terminating AD actions, the European Council can simply override this decision by qualified majority. In other trade-related matters, these actions would require qualified and unanimous decision making respectively. As a result, Eymann and Schuknecht (1993) find out that despite the decentralized AD administration, it has become the main instrument to control imports to the EU and that decisions inhibit a similar protectionist bias as those of the USA.

Only few scholars take into account the current trends of industrializing countries overtaking high-income nations in the usage of AD protection against both, developed as well as other developing countries (Kufuor 1998). Besides Messerlin's (2004) analysis of AD practices by and against China, another exception is the study by Niels and ten Kate (2004), analyzing Mexico's AD practices with the aim of identifying similarities to the high-income users. They find out that AD filings exhibit the same protectionist biases and contend that paradoxically

Mexican trade liberalization was only possible under the simultaneous increase in AD measures, which satisfy the protectionist demands of individual free-trade opponents. Focused AD protection serves as safety-belt for the effects of large scale liberalization.

In sum, contingent protection helps to appease domestic import-competitors confronted with WTO liberalization measures. The focuses application of anti-dumping measures to politically powerful industries hence reduces their opposition against broader WTO liberalization strategies. Chapter 4 extends this literature by analysing if WTO members do also react with contingent protection to the redistributive effects of WTO enlargement – again in the case of China's WTO accession. Throughout the 1990s, China has become the main target of AD measures. In 2001, the year of its WTO accession, almost 20% of world-wide antidumping measures have been imposed on Chinese products, and surprisingly, China has been targeted even more by developing countries than by industrial economies (Messerlin 2004; Niels and ten Kate 2004). Chapter 4 thus shows that WTO member states increase their AD activity against China towards the date of accession to appease domestic industries facing increasing Chinese competition. Contingent protection hence reduces the redistributive conflicts between losers and winners from China's integration into the world trade system: free-traders waiting for China to join the WTO, and protectionist industries fearing further increasing competition. The subtle and legal way of contingent protection allows governments to further protect domestic industries from the influx of Chinese goods *without* having to oppose the accession of China to the WTO.

2.4 The Research Gap

This book aims at analyzing the influence of redistributive effects from WTO enlargement on problems occurring in the accession process and on protectionist responses to new members. Consequentially, I draw on theories of international trade and protection to identify the winners and losers of trade liberalization, who are simultaneously the proponents of and opponents to WTO enlargement. The research desideratum of theories analyzing redistributive effects of moving from protectionism to free-trade is however their limitation to bilateral scenarios. Import-competitors oppose tariff reductions negotiated between two governments on a more or less reciprocal basis. In contrast, exporters welcome such a step towards free-trade as it opens up foreign markets. When a candidate country negotiates tariff reductions with each WTO member during the accession process, this logic holds for each bilaterally reached agreement, but not for their multilateralization. Reciprocal market access conditions negotiated between the candidate and any WTO member finally apply to all other members. Export-oriented industries profiting from improved market access to the candidate simultaneously have to compete with industries from other WTO countries, which received equal market access once the candidate joins the organization.

Export-, or third-market competition can lead to a situation in which not only import-competitors face negative redistributive income effects from trade liberalization, but also a fraction of exporters. Negative redistributive income effects for export-oriented industries occurring from multilateral trade liberalization has so far been underexposed in the literature on trade and protection, despite its profound consequences for individual WTO accessions. The more export-oriented industries are negatively affected by new members' third-market competition, the higher is the opposition to enlargement *in addition* to the resistance of import-competitors. In contrast to third-market competition, WTO governments have tools at hand to limit the opposition arising from import-competition.

As approaches in the field of the political economy of contingent protection show, antidumping measures applied to specific import-competing industries are especially helpful for reducing the opposition against broader liberalization measures. Thus, even if government fully commit to WTO liberalization demands, antidumping regulations remain as a subtle form of protectionism. As such, this approach is also capable of explaining increasing antidumping measures against WTO candidates as a protectionist response to their membership ambitions. Surprisingly, no such approach exists. This is mainly due to the fact that approaches on contingent protection are user biased: they mainly focus on individual industrial countries' utilization of antidumping measures against other WTO members. Chapter 4 fills this gap by analyzing why one WTO candidate – China – was increasingly targeted with contingent protection by a multitude of developing, newly industrialized and high-income economies during its accession process.

The argument is straightforward. Import-competitors of many WTO countries feared the influx of cheap Chinese goods with the tariff reductions broad along with its membership. As a result, import-competitors opposed China's accession. Governments were thus caught in between redistributive conflicts between proponents of and opponents to China's accession. As the accession negotiations progressed and the probability of China joining the organization increased, governments searched for alternative possibilities to protect their influential import-competitors and increasingly fostered national antidumping regulation. This way, governments could promote China's accession to the advantage of free-traders, while simultaneously offering focused protection to the redistributive losers from China's economic integration.

Chapter 5 examines the so far underexplored phenomenon of third-market competition. While governments can solve redistributive conflicts for import-competitors by contingent protection, they are powerless if large fractions of their exporters are confronted with international third-market competition. If third-market competition arises from WTO enlargement, the only possibility to prolong exporters' international quota rents vis-à-vis the candidates' competitors is to delay the accession of the prospective member.

Hence, the remainder of this book offers a sound explanation of how redistributive effects caused by trade liberalization measures prior WTO enlargement influence governments' preferences in accession negotiations and how they solve conflicting interests between industries favouring new countries to the WTO and those who do not. But before delving into how governments reduce the threat of increasing import-competition by means of antidumping against China in the initial analysis, I first provide more background information on the WTO accession process and explain the selection of China's WTO accession as a crucial case for analyzing the hypothesized relations.

3   WTO ENLARGEMENT: FACTS AND FIGURES

When the WTO came into being in 1995 with the signing of the Marrakech agreement, 128 countries either became founding WTO members or rejoined the organization shortly after its foundation. More then 50 developing, newly industrialized and transition countries, all of which had also been GATT outsiders were excluded from the new developments in the world trade system.[2] Since 1995 these formerly excluded nations seek entry to the WTO and 21 have already been successful, including China and Saudi Arabia. Another 31 countries are currently negotiating their integration into liberalized world trade, among them Russia and the Ukraine. In short: nearly every existing country seeks WTO membership.[3]

The problem of the WTO heading towards universal membership is that with every new member the accession process becomes increasingly cumbersome due to the large number of trade related interests to be considered. Because the WTO is a member driven organization, individual interests can have a significant impact on further enlargement. For a better understanding of the redistributive conflicts and their influence on the accession process, this chapter explains the goods provided by the WTO to its members, the resulting incentives of non-members to join the organization, the characteristics of the accession process and the working parties, and finally the selection of China as a crucial case for the analysis of the redistributive conflicts' influence on the accession process.

The description of the accession process reveals that WTO membership is mostly subject to negotiations among members and candidates. New WTO members join the organization at 'the terms to be agreed'. Due to this vague nature of accession rules, causing trouble during the accession process is a walkover for anti-integrationist governments. In sum, the background information of this chapter provides first insights on the bold venture of integrating China into the world trade system by means of this negotiation-based accession procedure.

---

[2] See WTO homepage at http://www.wto.org/english/thewto_e/gattmem_e.htm.
[3] See the WTO Accession Gateway at http://www.wto.org/English/thewto_e/acc_e/acc_e.htm.

3.1 WTO Membership Benefits

As the WTO heads towards universal membership, the number of worldwide WTO outsiders shrinks. In the past 12 years, 21 countries have joined the organization and 21 more are in the process of joining.[4] What are the motives of these developing, newly industrialized or transition economies to seek entry to the trade club? Motives to join the WTO are manifold – both economically as well as politically. First, the Most Favoured Nation principle (MFN) guarantees that bilaterally negotiated trade conditions e.g. in the form of tariff reductions be granted to the universe of WTO members. From an economic perspective, this is the most prominent motive for outsiders to apply for accession. By entering the organization, new members can access all other members' markets at conditions other members had to bargain for in numerous previous liberalization rounds (Hoekman and Kostecki 2001). This form of attractiveness hence increases with the membership size of the WTO – or, in other words: the costs of being an outsider with limited market access to the bulk of WTO countries increases with every trading partner entering the organization.

In these terms, applicants fear that the devil takes the hindmost, especially if neighbouring trade partners enter the organization. At the same time, old members are likely to demand stricter accession conditions with increasing membership size simply because the advantage of being a club member disappears without outsiders. Members are members because they strive for a competitive advantage compared to non-members. Benefits from being a WTO member must be regarded as a club good, which is per definition excludable. When WTO membership reaches universality, excludability vanishes and free-trade and dispute-settlement benefits turn into a common good. While this is clearly the objective of the WTO secretariat, it should be doubted that it is also the wish of individual members. With universal membership, the incentives to discriminate each other within the organization rise - especially if old members fear that new members, all of which are either transformation- newly industrialized- or developing economies, could free-ride on previously made tariff concessions (Bond et al. 2000).

---

[4] The 21 'new' members are Albania (joined in 2000), Armenia (2003), Bulgaria (1996), Cambodia (1994), the People's Republic of China (2001), Chinese Taipei (2002), Croatia (2000), Ecuador (1996), Estonia (1999), Georgia (2000), Jordan (2000), Kyrgyz Republic (1998), Latvia (1999), Lithuania (2001), FYR Macedonia (2003), Moldova (2001), Mongolia (1997), Nepal (2004), Oman (2000), Panama (1997), and Saudi Arabia (2005) (WTO 2004).

The second incentive to join the organization is closely connected to improved trade conditions in goods and services. Membership enables governments to take legal actions against trading partners infringing WTO trade rules and the doctrine of non-discrimination before the dispute settlement body. Countries joining the WTO gain legal certainty within the international trade system. Numerous rules on anti-dumping and safeguard practices additionally allows Members to counteract dumping practices by other Members as well as by outsiders. Despite all liberalization pressures, WTO rules still allow new members to protect individual domestic industries if they face injury due to dumped imports.

Third, governments striving for domestic reform, which applies to the majority of the transition and developing economies that have acceded the WTO since 1995, profit from WTO trade regime requirements to strengthen their domestic bargaining position vis-à-vis reform-reluctant groups. The WTO hence provides governments with the possibility to lock-in domestic reform necessities against the will of opposing interests and, moreover, with technical assistance and guidance towards more liberal trade policies, reduction of state trading entities and subsidies, and the establishment of a legal system guaranteeing contract certainty (Michalopoulos 1998). Vice versa and analogous to Putnam's (1988) logic of two-level-games, governments not willing to satisfy accession conditions with respect to domestic trade regime reform utilize reluctant domestic interests to strengthen their bargaining position in the accession process.

Clearly, the gains at stake from WTO membership vary among applicant countries with individual country characteristics. Small economies in transition with only low trade volumes can be expected to be more interested into reform assistance for their domestic trade regime than in foreign tariff liberalization. In contrast, more export oriented newly industrialized countries would benefit from improved foreign market access with WTO membership. Again others need access to the dispute settlement body to reduce costly trade conflicts. In any case: the gains at stake for these countries determine their opportunity costs of being WTO outsiders.

Ironically, the complexity of the accession process also increases with the gains at stake. The more important a country is in terms of international trade, the more bilateral trade agreements need to be finalized before accession. For a better understanding of this crucial relation, the next section offers a brief description of the WTO accession process. It especially explains how the WTO accession procedure supplies opposing countries with sufficient leverage to slow down negotiations. The core of the accession constitutes bilateral market access negotiations. To join, the applicant must conduct negotiations with every interested member. By delaying individual bilateral negotiations, opposing members can block the entire membership.

3.2 The Accession Process: It's All About Bilateral Relations

The WTO accession process is complex – not because of all-embracing rule types, but because of the opposite: a majority of the terms to be agreed upon are subject to numerous negotiations among WTO members and the applicant. The vague institutional design forms the platform for lengthy and member driven accession negotiations. This section sketches the basis accession provisions, followed by a description of the formation of the Working Party (WP) to the Accession of New Members and its role for membership negotiations. The WP is a committee composed of all WTO member states interested in applicants' membership conditions. Stated simply, members participate in the work of the WP because they have either gains or losses at stake from WTO membership of the respective applicant.

Before further delving into the significance of the WP, major accession provisions reveal their vague character. Article XII of the WTO founding Marrakech Agreement basically regulates the WTO accession process by referring back to the original GATT 1947 accession clauses. More precisely, Article XII states that:

"1. Any State or separate customs territory possessing full autonomy in the conduct of its external commercial relations and of the other matters provided for in this Agreement and the Multilateral Trade Agreements may accede to this Agreement, on terms to be agreed between it and the WTO. Such accession shall apply to this Agreement and the Multilateral Trade Agreements annexed thereto.

2. Decisions on accession shall be taken by the Ministerial Conference. The Ministerial Conference shall approve the agreement on the terms of accession by a two-thirds majority of the Members of the WTO." (WTO n.d.).

In a nutshell, these Articles provide every interested country with the right to enter the organizations on individually negotiated terms with all other members of the WTO. With respect to more precise rules and procedures, Article XVI of the Marrakech agreement clarifies that:

"Except as otherwise provided under this Agreement or the Multilateral Trade Agreements, the WTO shall be guided by the decisions, procedures and customary practices followed by the CONTRACTING PARTIES to GATT 1947 and the bodies established in the framework of GATT 1947." (WTO 1995).

Hence, acceding to the WTO does not differ much from historical GATT accessions. This original accession procedure, as laid out in Article XXXIII of GATT 1947 (WTO 1995), is illustrated in Figure 3.1.

The procedure can be summarized as follows. The request for accession by the applicant country, which is distributed to all members, is followed by the formation of a Working Party (WP). The WP is the central body for the determination of membership requirements, that is 'the terms to be agreed' (WTO 1995) and the supervision of their implementation. Countries participating in the WP are therefore the most important negotiators in the accession process and also the key actors of the upcoming analysis of China's accession to the WTO. The government applying for membership submits a memorandum to WP members containing detailed information on all aspects of domestic trade policies. The resulting transparency of the applicant's trade regime serves as a foundation for necessary concessions demanded by old members.

The core part of the accession process starts subsequently with two simultaneous procedures. The working party studies the memorandum submitted and examines the conformity of the applicants' trade policies with WTO membership rules. On this basis, the WP designs the terms and conditions on the applicants accession. But more important within the frame of this analysis are the simultaneously conducted bilateral negotiations concerning the concessions on goods and services. While the administrative process of the WP is reviewing the applicant's trade system, each interested WP member is welcome to negotiate individual trade liberalization measures in the form of market access exchange in goods and services with the applicant.

Figure 3.1   The WTO Accession Process

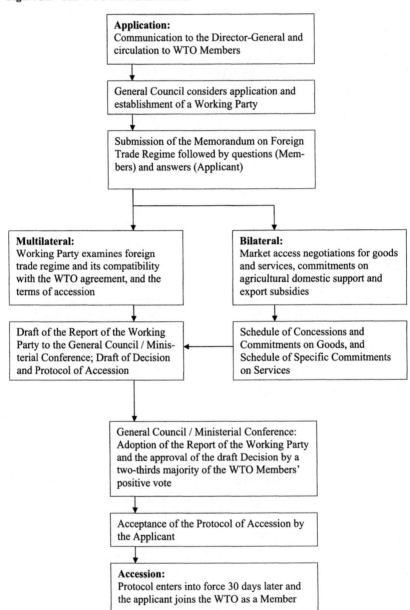

Bilateral negotiations are important for several reasons for both the pace as well as for the outcome of the accession process. First, bilateral negotiations are time consuming. The length of WTO accessions is therefore naturally a function of the number of members engaged in bilateral negotiations. Second, while formally "The Ministerial Conference shall approve the agreement on the terms of accession by a two-thirds majority of the Members of the WTO" (WTO 1995: Article XII, 2), accession will not be subject to this decision unless the WP has concluded its work, which is unlikely to happen before each of the WP members have reached an agreement with the applicant. In other words, although the final decision is subject to a two-third majority, each WP member can delay the final decision by not reaching bilateral agreements with the candidate government.

Outcomes of the bilaterally negotiated agreements are merged into the candidate's schedule of concessions and commitments on goods as well as into the respective schedule on services. If WP members are satisfied with the progress of the applicant's trade regime reform, and if the schedules of concessions have been submitted to the WP, it adopts a draft report. The adoption of the accession protocol and the WP report is finally subject to a two-thirds majority by the General Council and the Ministerial Conference. Again, the requirement of the two-thirds majority is merely a formality. The WP seldom issues a draft report unless most of the conflicting accession interests are smoothed out.

Thus while individual countries are not able to veto accession at the last stage, they can do so by retarding bilateral negotiations since the WP will not provide the necessary draft before bilateral market access talks have been concluded. For this reason, the composition of the working party and the progress of bilateral talks are essential for accession conditions and new and old members' utility from organizational enlargement. WP composition hints towards the crucial negotiators of new WTO members and it can generally be assumed that WP members either oppose accession, or benefit from new members. Countries not participating in accession talks can analogously be expected to be indifferent about respective enlargements. The next section discusses the size of individual WPs since 1995, including the WP to the accession of China, in relation to negotiation durations. China's WP has by far been the largest. Due its countries' favouring or opposing interests towards China becoming a WTO member, the WP to the accession of China forms the sample for later analysis.

3.3 Working Party Composition

The Working Party (WP) is of central importance for the accession conditions of new members and consequentially also for the distributive effects of WTO enlargement between new and old, as well as between respective old members. This is due to the fact that WTO member governments interested in affecting accession conditions of future members are welcome to negotiate the concessions demanded and the rights granted in the case of a candidate's acceptance. On the one hand, the WP accommodates the candidate's trading partners, which aim at negotiating the candidate's tariff concessions for increasing gains from future trade. On the other hand, member governments opposing the candidate's accession for protectionist motives are also likely to participate in the Working Party to limit membership rights or – in the worst case – to block the accession process.

WP members thus form the core of the negotiations. They are commonly also the countries interested in the central bilateral market access negotiations with the candidate. While in formal WP meetings the general terms of accession must be agreed upon, individual tariff schedules of new members and the degree of reciprocal liberalization is more or less subject to bilateral talks. The impact of WP members on the membership conditions of candidates is therefore twofold. The requirement to finalize bilateral talks among WP members and the applicant before possible enlargement further increases the bargaining power of WP members in the accession process. If old members are not satisfied with the concessions offered by applicants, they can credibly threaten to delay negotiations.

The size of individual Working Parties varies with the accession candidate. While 44 of 62 WP members participated in the trade negotiation process of China's accession, only 15 tried to affect membership conditions of e.g. the Kyrgyz Republic, which joined in 1998 after the shortest accession period of only two years (Gertler 2003; Kennett et al. 2005). Australia, Canada, the European Union and its Member States, India, Japan, New Zealand, Switzerland and the United States form the core group participating in almost every WP.

The WP to the accession of China thereby forms the intersection of countries, which have generally attended one or more other accession Working Parties (Kennett et al. 2005). Table 3.1 summarizes the new WTO members since 1995 with information concerning their accession process. It shows that not only the size of the working party varies significantly, but also the duration from the date of its formation to accession.[5]

Table 3.1 New WTO Members since 1995

Country	Date of WP Establishment	Date of Accession	WP Duration (years)	WP Size (no. of countries)
Albania	1992	2000	8	16
Armenia	1993	2003	10	30
Bulgaria	1990	1996	6	22
Cambodia	1994	2004	10	15
China	1987	2001	14	62
Chinese Taipei	1992	2002	10	48
Croatia	1993	2000	7	19
Ecuador	1992	1996	4	21
Estonia	1994	1999	5	21
Georgia	1996	2000	4	21
Jordan	1994	2000	6	32
Kyrgyz Republic	1996	1998	2	15
Latvia	1993	1999	6	24
Lithuania	1994	2001	7	27
FYR Macedonia	1994	2003	9	23
Moldova	1993	2001	8	25
Mongolia	1991	1997	6	17
Nepal	1999	2004	5	23
Oman	1996	2000	4	31
Panama	1991	1997	6	34
Saudi Arabia	1993	2005	12	nn

Source: UNCTAD 2001, Kennett et al. (2005)

While WP members worked 14 years to integrate China into the world trade system, the Kyrgyz Republic joined after only two years; Ecuador, Georgia and Oman after 4 years of negotiations. Since the WP of China's accession was by far the largest with 62 members, one could speculate that accession duration is simply a function of WP size.

Figure 3.2 plots WP size against the duration of its work. Besides a few outliers such as the Kyrgyz Republic, Chinese Taipei and China, a linear relationship between WP size and duration does not hold true. While for example Panama

---

[5] Note that the foundation of the working party is not equivalent to the start of the accession procedure. The People's Republic of China for instance already applied in 1986. One year past until the application was submitted to all members and the WP could be founded.

and Oman faced relatively large working parties, they nevertheless joined the organization within 6 and 4 years respectively. Cambodia's accession took in contrast 10 years with only 15 WP members.

Figure 3.2 Working Party Size and Accession Duration

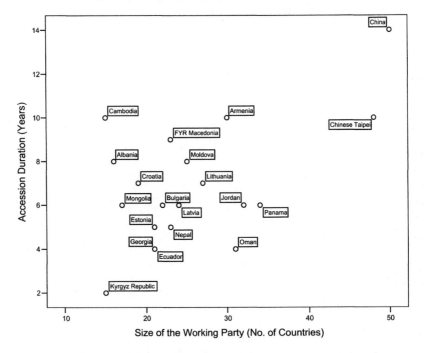

The pure number of WP members hence seems to be a merely weak indicator for accession durations. Although the WP size indicates the overall interest in new memberships, one problematic negotiation dyad is theoretically sufficient to protract the entire accession process. For illustration consider the new WTO member Cambodia compared to the Kyrgyz Republic – two countries in transition with significant political turmoil up to the 1990s. In both cases, 15 WTO members participated in the respective WPs to negotiate membership conditions. In the case of the Kyrgyz Republic, no conflictual issues appeared and all WP members quickly reached bilateral agreements with the Kyrgyz government – otherwise it would not have been possible to integrate the new member in two years only.

In contrast, conflictual issues must have appeared in Cambodia's accession negotiations, which required 10 years to accede to the organization. However, this does not mean that Cambodia's government was in conflict about trade policy issues with *all* 15 WP members. Theoretically, contentious trade policy issues with only one or two WP members about 'the terms to be agreed' would be sufficient to delay the accession process. Hence, conflicts in individual negotiation dyads can be decisive determinants for the length of individual accession procedures. The analysis of contentious negotiation issues must be a main focus when analyzing WTO enlargement. If conflicts arise especially in bilateral market access negotiations as a consequence of redistributive effects, the date of accession can significantly be delayed as will be shown for China's accession in Chapter 5.

This underlines that the success of joining the WTO cannot only be attributed to national governments' willingness to make large scale economic reforms and market opening; thus bringing former centrally planned economies in line with WTO rules (Broude 1998; Langhammer and Lücke 1999; Michalopoulos 1998; Yang 1999). Instead, internal stumbling blocs to WTO accession can only fully account for the length of the accession process if all other members generally support the respective candidate's membership. As soon as other WTO members oppose the integration of a new member to the WTO, although the candidate implements all reform requirements, institutional obstacles and reform reluctance cannot solely explain a variation in countries' accession durations.

China's accession to the WTO demonstrates that especially if candidates are economically important, their organizational integration is likely to affect old members' trade relations in one way or the other, triggering redistributive conflicts both domestically and between members. The number of countries opposing the accession of a new country increases with the trade power of the candidate and the threat of competition accompanied by its integration into the world trade system. In other words, while for small, non-trading developing and transition economies purely internal reform obstacles might account for their accession length, external factors in the form of opposing WTO members additionally slow down the accession process of economically more powerful nations such as China, Russia, or Saudi Arabia.

The next section directs special attention to the People's Republic of China, which constitutes a crucial case and founds the centre of this book's empirical parts: With its growing economic power, China is – among all accessions since 1995 – suited best to theorize and illustrate the redistributive effects of the multilateral WTO enlargement process.

3.4 Case Selection: China and the WTO

The People's Republic of China is – among all new and currently negotiating prospective WTO members – the nation which faced the highest opportunity costs of not being a GATT/WTO member until its accession in 2001. First and foremost, China is a fast growing and export oriented economy, losing from higher foreign market access costs as an outsider. Second, as a WTO member, China's government could avert a number of protectionist measures imposed by WTO member states before the dispute settlement body. Third, membership requirements in the WTO push China towards a rule based and market oriented economy, which also positively impacts its economic growth. The accession process thus helps Chinese officials to lock-in economic reforms, possibly against the will of domestic interest groups (Yang 2000). Fourth, all countries competing with China on a large scale for international market shares in exports are WTO members.

But while the benefits for China are so prevalent, the accession process took 15 years because its economic strength triggered at the same time a number of redistributive conflicts for old WTO members, which stand in the centre of upcoming analyses. Thus, China's WTO accession is extremely well suited to explain how redistributive conflicts hamper the enlargement of multilateral trade agreements and the WTO. China is nevertheless a crucial and a lonely case simply because its economic significance coupled with its WTO outsider status throughout the 1990s is incomparable. The logic is nevertheless applicable to other countries and trade agreements: the competition powerful traders cause for members of a trade agreement and the consequential redistributive effects are inversely related to the probability of a quick enlargement. The remainder of this section introduces key Chinese characteristics, which underlie the importance of this case.

China's benefits from joining the WTO are closely connected to its rapid economic growth, which is partly due to far reaching domestic structural reforms since the early 1980s. Despite being a communist state, the People's Republic of

China managed to turn a centrally planned into a market based economy, at least with respect to trade policies. For this achievement, the early years of reform have brought more disentanglement between the government and enterprises and the removal of price controls. With its application to join GATT in 1986, Chinese officials started more radical reforms in line with GATT requirements such as the privatization of state-owned enterprises (SOE), reform of the banking sector, reduction of non-tariff barriers and with increasing bilateral trade agreements also the cutting of import-tariffs (Song 2003). While these changes are remarkable, Yang (2000) points out that

"The system is full of inconsistencies but short of transparency and rationality. (...) Trade measures are hardly exposed to public debate so most people would not have a clue about the trade restrictions on various commodities. Tariffs and other barriers are often changed and their application depends on who the importer is. Information on trade regulations is often not available in the public domain. This is also the main focus of complaints by China's trading partners about the lack of transparency in the trade regime. Greater transparency in the trade regime will also have profound implications for the rest of the economy. In particular, it sets the course for reform of the SOE sector and helps establish rule-based domestic institutions. These trickle-down effects are likely to be substantial." (Yang 2000: 11).

In sum, China has indeed conducted a wide range of reforms, but transparency of the trade regime remains to be a critical issue. Moreover, Chinese officials managed the turn to a market-based, but not yet fully to a rule-based economy, a circumstance especially uttered in the discussion on the protection of intellectual property rights.

Despite such remedies, the reforms are all the more impressive when considering the domestic forces opposing domestic privatization, liberalization and the opening of the market. Service industries such as banking, telecommunications and insurance have for instance been dominated by SOEs. The same applies to heavy industries such as steel or chemicals. Due to their low degree of efficiency and weak financial performance, their privatization causes unemployment, which supplies industrial interest groups with sufficient leverage to oppose ongoing reform measures (Yang 2000: 14). However, the WTO prescribes the liberalization of Chinese SOEs for accession, allowing Chinese government officials to divert the responsibility for job losses in former state-owned enterprises

to the WTO secretariat. This way, WTO accession requirements serve to domestically enforce necessary reforms against opposing interest groups.

Without market oriented reform measures, the accelerated growth of the Chinese
economy would have hardly been possible. From 1990 to 2002, China's GDP
quadrupled from $ 1480 to $ 5860 billion and exports and imports sextupled
from roughly $ 50 to $ 300 billion respectively. Domestic economic reform also
turned China into an attractive market for foreign investors. In only seven years,
from 1990 to 1996, net FDI inflows increased form $ 3.5 billion to $ 40 billion,
before they stagnated at this level. Despite these upwards rocketing economic
indicators, China remains a fairly poor country although GDP per capita significantly increased from $ 1310 in 1990 to $ 4580 in 2002 (World Bank 2004).

Given the increasing volume of international trade from and to China, and its
importance for the Chinese economy, it seems astonishing that China could exist
outside the WTO until 2001. However, the crux for China – so one of the main
arguments – is that while it would largely benefit from membership, its increasing trade power does also impact the competitive status quo on international
markets which triggers conflicts with WTO members.

In short: China's benefits from membership are positively correlated with the
conflicts it causes. Chapter 2 demonstrated that in previous research the attention has traditionally been focused on conflicts emerging from increased international competition in one of the largest Chinese export industries: textiles and
clothing (e.g. Dickson 2003, Shafaeddin, 2002). Industrial nations fear the influx
of cheap Chinese textiles, which contest import-competing industries. Textiles
exporters, e.g. India and Pakistan, on the other hand face losses of international
market shares to Chinese producers. However, while China is doubtlessly a
powerful exporter of textiles and clothing, these industries' role for emerging
conflict is slightly overrated for two reasons.

First, international trade in textiles and clothing was, until 1994, governed by the
Multifibre Arrangement (MFA), supplying especially industrialized countries
with numerous possibilities to regulate textiles flows in their interest. In 1995,
the MFA was replaced by the Agreement on Textiles and Clothing (ATC) aimed
at phasing out textiles regulation by 2005. Being subject to the ATC, China's
textile exports have been regulated up to four years past its accession. Moreover,
provisions in China's accession protocol grant other WTO members the right to
further impose discriminatory safeguards and anti-dumping measures on Chi-

nese goods. One of these measures allows members to further restrict imports of textiles covered by the ATC up to four years after its official phase out, that is, up to December 2008 (Dickson 2003). The competitive threat emerging from Chinese textiles and clothing industries is hence already limited by formal accession provisions.

Second, and probably more important for long-term competition issues, China's textile industry is also economically overrated when considering changes in its export structure. For visualization, Figure 3.3 plots the developments of four industries which make up the lion's share of Chinese exports: iron and steel, chemicals, textiles and clothing as well as more capital intense products of office and telecommunication equipment.

Figure 3.3 China's Industry-Specific Export Growth 1990-2004

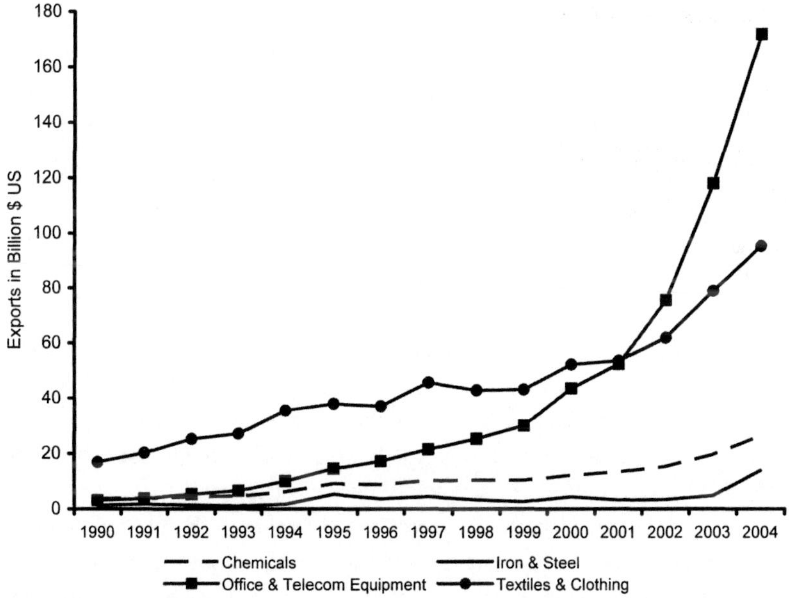

Source: WTO Trade Statistics

It is evident that textiles and clothing have in fact been China's most important export industries – throughout the 1990s. This picture changes exactly in 2001 –

the year of accession – when more capital intense products of the office and telecommunication family take over the leading role in Chinese exports. From then on, export volumes for office, telecommunication and computer products tripled up to almost \$ 180 billion in 2004. Even without further restrictions, it seems unlikely that textiles and clothing exports would have reached a comparable accelerated growth.

China remains a powerful exporter of textiles, but is simultaneously developing capacities for the production of more capital intense manufactured goods. This change in comparative advantage is of special importance for conflict lines among China and old members in the accession negotiations, which is subject to later analysis. This first introduction to China's export strength and variety indicates that not only countries dominated by labour intense industries are inclined to oppose its accession due to the fear of increasing competition, but also more advanced economies specialized in the production of more capital intense goods which exhibit large growth rates in China.

Hence, while emerging competition for international textiles producers constitutes a critical point in China's accession negotiations, the upcoming analyses will also demonstrate that the growing export diversity creates a wider circle of countries opposing its integration than just those fearing contestation of textiles producers.

The next Chapter alludes to the first line of conflict in China's WTO accession negotiations: Governments which are heavily influenced by domestic import-competing industries will promote China's accession less than governments not facing domestic constraints. Those governments whose import-competitors are adversely affected by China's WTO accession can nevertheless solve this dilemma by increasing 'contingent protection', that is, by applying focused anti-dumping measures to those Chinese goods which challenge domestic producers. This enables governments to supply special industries with contingent protection, while negotiating improved access to Chinese markets for exporters. The empirical test shows that antidumping measures indeed have increasingly been filed against China in the course of its accession negotiations by especially those countries with high Chinese import-penetration ratios.

4 REDISTRIBUTIVE CONFLICTS I:
IMPORT-COMPETITION AND CONTINGENT PROTECTION

Extensive trade liberalization measures conducted in the course of WTO accession negotiations bear far reaching consequences for domestic industries of old WTO member states as well as of applicant countries. The most prominent losers of domestic tariff reductions are import-competing producers: the reduction of import tariffs lowers the costs for foreign companies to sell their products abroad. Competing domestic industries and individual factor owners attached to them inevitably face income losses through the adjustment of prices to the new competitive situation.

The crucial example of China fighting for its integration into the world trade system illustrates the fear of domestic industries and their national governments of increasing Chinese import-competition and the consequential redistributive income effects. On its long way to the WTO, China faced significant protectionist responses to its membership ambitions. Arguing that the transformation from a centrally planned to a market-based economy had not been entirely completed by the date of accession and being sceptical that a communist government will not intervene in liberal trade policies in the long run, member states managed to implement protective safeguard measures into China's protocol of accession.

This existing demand for ongoing trade distorting measures against Chinese goods is reflected in numerous empirical research approaches, triggered by China's 15 year long accession process and its accelerated economic growth. Articles mainly focus on the redistributive consequences of China's accession for other members, caused by the increasing competition in labour intense manufactured goods and especially textiles and clothing (Evans 2004; Ianchovichina and Walmsley 2005; Lardy 2002; Shafaeddin 2002; Sussangkarn 2004; Wang 2003).[6] Reacting to the increasing competition on world markets caused by Chinese producers, established WTO members negotiated a number of safeguard clauses to be introduced into the official accession protocol to limit the stress of competition. Scholars commonly agree that such special safeguard clauses limit China's membership rights beyond its accession in 2001, securing other exporters a competitive advantage vis-à-vis China (Mallon and Whalley

---

[6] Please see also the more general survey on WTO- and China-specific research in Chapter 2.

2004; Rumbaugh and Blancher 2004; Walmsley and Hertel 2000; Wang 2000; Yang 1999).

Eventually, the Chinese government had no choice but to accept these ongoing trade restrictions to finally accede to the WTO, which "... opens the flood gate for discriminatory measures against China and potentially for all transition economies seeking WTO accession in the future" (Yang 1999: 528).[7]

Beyond official safeguards and 'differentiated membership' (Schneider 2005), mainly in the form of ongoing import quotas or tariffs, China's economic growth and accession to the WTO was expected to exert a significant increase in competitive pressures for domestic industries of other WTO members. As the redistributive conflicts of increasing import-competition are not solely a function of its economic growth but also of the liberalization measures accompanied by China's WTO accession, the fear of income redistribution also triggered political conflicts in WTO accession negotiations. This chapter deals with the solution to these political conflicts, that is, it explains how protectionist WTO members manage to reduce import-competition, without having to oppose the entire accession process.

More specifically, I argue that a second mechanism further weakened overt protectionism against China in the accession process in addition to officially implemented safeguards: the vague definition and the loopholes inherent to WTO antidumping (AD) procedures allow governments to supply industries with 'contingent protection' (Tharakan 1995; Messerlin and Tharakan 2000) or 'administered protection' (Baldwin 1998), without having to oppose WTO membership of important applicants such as China. Consequentially, reluctant governments could utilize antidumping measures as substitutes for traditional tariff applied to WTO outsiders. This subtle protectionist response to WTO membership ambitions enabled old members' governments to satisfy protectionist industries opposing enlargement without infringing on the WTO doctrine of nondiscrimination. The concept of 'contingent protection' is not novel, but it has commonly been used for the analysis of mainly industrial economies as users of AD measures to appease import-competing industries with AD measures, while liberalizing trade for exporters. This research has so far however not analyzed why a wide range of countries – developing and developed – increasingly file

---

[7] In the case of EU enlargement, restricting membership rights of new members to appease accession opponents is commonly known as 'differentiated membership' (e.g. Schneider 2005).

antidumping measures against one target country.[8] This chapter focuses on a WTO candidate – using China as an example – as a main target of antidumping, undermining its membership rights past accession. It proceeds as follows.

The upcoming theoretical part within this chapter explains that AD filings first reduce conflicting domestic interests between import-competitors and free-traders with respect to trade liberalization measures of WTO enlargement. The focussed application of AD measures to industries otherwise losing from trade liberalization minimizes their opposition and allows for negotiating liberal policies to the advantage of winning exporters. Second and closely related to this, contingent protection also minimizes interstate conflicts between member governments promoting WTO enlargement and those who oppose it. The magnitude of antidumping measures is expected to be determined by industries' significance in the form of size and labour intensity and by the probability of the candidate's accession. This is due to the fact that members are forced to reduce their traditional trade barriers by the date of accession. The more realistic the candidate's membership, the more WTO members have to be concerned with applying alternative protection such as antidumping measures.

The empirical test using China as a crucial case finally indicates that especially three factors exert a significant impact on the magnitude of contingent protection against China during accession negotiations. First, the relative size of domestically affected industries and their import penetration ratio from China is positively related to the probability of receiving antidumping protection. Second, members' fear of Chinese retaliation past its accession reduces the probability of antidumping measures. Finally, protectionist responses to China's future WTO membership increase over time during the 15 year long accession negotiations.

4.1 Theory: Protectionist Responses to WTO Enlargement

The subsequent theoretical considerations explain the emergence of conflicts among China – representing an important new trading nation within the WTO – and protectionist countries, which fear increasing competition for domestic producers with trade liberalization measures in the course of WTO accessions.

---

[8] Please see Chapter 2 for a discussion of approaches dealing with anti-dumping practices and contingent protection.

More specifically, the theory of the political economy of contingent and administered protection offers a solution to this conflict with respect to WTO enlargement: the utilization of AD for protectionist purposes against a candidate enables WTO governments to diminish competition for individual industries, without having to oppose new members to the organization. Employing AD duties on specific imports is a growing and widely accepted tool of 'contingent protection' for WTO member countries (Tharakan 1995). The vague definition of what constitutes dumping and the intransparency of individual countries' price settings for special industries enables other governments to file antidumping measures even if price settings are not manipulated and trade distorting. Furthermore, AD rules contain loopholes which allow their application of if dumped imports do in fact *not* economically injure domestic industries (Tharakan 1995).

Contingent protection is common practice among many WTO Members, but the focal point of this analysis is its application against forthcoming members to limit the redistributive economic impact of their accession on domestic producers. Knowing that a candidate's economic growth coupled with the liberalized trade within the WTO will increase competition for both import- and export-competing industries, it is argued that governments put more effort into the search for alternative protective tools with a rising probability of the applicant's entry. From a political economy point of view, this is explained by the circumstance that governments are caught in-between the interests of domestic consumers and exporters gaining from enlargement and those producers facing increasing competition. The most efficient solution for governments to satisfy both interests is to support accession and thereby negotiate trade liberalization for the free-trade oriented industries, while simultaneously utilizing antidumping measures to further offer protection for import- and export-competing interests.

The two alternatives to contingent protection are pareto inferior for the simple reason that both upset either side of the interests. If governments would agree to unconditional accession with full market access for the candidate, they suffer vote losses from the electorate employed in uncompetitive industries. If, on the other hand, governments would fully veto accession, they risk losing votes from large fractions of the electorate employed in export-oriented industries plus consumers. Supporting accession, but protecting the fraction of the electorate employed in otherwise loosing industries through antidumping measures secures votes from both sides.

This mechanism is thereby expected to be a function of the accession likelihood during negotiations. As long as the accession appears to be unlikely and the outsider status of the candidate is stable, governments do not need to establish alternative protectionist barriers since normal tariffs are in place against nonmembers. However, as more and more WP members conclude bilateral market access negotiations with the applicant government, the probability of a near accession increases. In addition, the more old governments conclude bilateral talks, the more difficult it becomes for individual opposing governments to justify their protectionist sentiments – both at home and among other WTO Member governments. Consequentially, contingent protection against forthcoming members must be expected to increase during the final bilateral negotiation phase.

Note that not every AD duty filed against imports is generally abused for protectionism. The crux of the WTO AD regulation is the indivisibility of justified and unjustified filings. In other words, it is difficult to determine if industries seek antidumping protection to counteract a trade-distorting foreign price setting, or if they demand antidumping protection to cause trade-distortions themselves for rent-seeking. Willig (1998) even considers a situation of 'strategic dumping' in which the protection of home markets "...makes possible the profitable setting of higher net prices at home than are charged for exports" (Willig 1998: 65). This situation is theoretically applicable to domestic corporations with large domestic as well as foreign market shares, that is, they are simultaneously export-oriented as well as import-competing. Their national government levies tariffs on competing imports, possibly in the form of AD, for which the given firm can hold the domestic price for its goods above its world market prices. The tariff rents they achieve on the domestic market through contingent protection are diverted to lower the prices of their export products internationally slightly below world market prices to increase their foreign sales. In sum, they apply measures of contingent protection to dump their exports in return.

Having clarified the general theoretical concept of contingent protection, what are – more specifically – the loopholes in AD regulations enabling national industries and governments to arbitrarily use them for the restriction of imports? The rules for the applicability of AD measures are contained in Article VI of GATT 1994. Accordingly, "... a product is to be considered as being dumped, i.e. introduced into the commerce of another country at less than its normal value, if the export price of the product exported from one country to another is less than the comparable price, in the ordinary course of trade, for the like product when destined for consumption in the exporting country" (WTO 1994: Article 2.1).

However, the determination of an appropriate comparable price, at which products would *not* be considered being dumped, is of such a hypothetical nature, that dumping is often found to be the case if domestic prices of complaining industries are simply higher than those of the 'dumped' imports. As Prusa (2001: 2) points out in this respect "AD is a trade policy where the filing, the legal decision, and the protective impact are endogenous. A foreign industry can almost guarantee it will not be subject to AD duties if it charges sufficiently high prices on its export markets. On the other hand, a domestic industry might resist lowering its prices because doing so improves its chances of winning an AD case."

Moreover, especially new users of AD do not provide the necessary transparency in their determination calculations for foreign and comparable prices (Prusa 2001: 8). This further underlines the suspicion that the dumping determination process is a rather arbitrary process of national authorities, which formally should be autonomous from national governments. De facto this is hard to guarantee. And even if they are independent and unbiased with respect to the demand of contingent protection by special industries, politicians – local or national, depending on the electoral system – can still provide industries with advice and assistance on *how* to file antidumping cases to maximize the probability of their acceptance by national AD authorities.

For the justification of AD measures national authorities must further prove that imports satisfying the above mentioned criteria do in fact injure domestic industries (WTO, 1994: Article 3). While the definition of dumping is already vague, the injury determination procedure provides national authorities with sufficient leeway to promote AD, even if industries are de facto not seriously harmed, as highlighted by Messerlin and Tharakan (1999: 1257). National authorities do not need to prove a causal impact of vaguely defined dumped imports on e.g. a rising unemployment rate of domestic industries for AD justification. Instead, the coexistence of dumped imports of like products and the industry specific downturn is sufficient for bringing about contingent protection. Or, referring back to the endogenous problem of AD decisions, an industry seeking AD protection can lay-off workers to indicate injury and thus to enhance the likelihood for protection.

Consequentially, WTO member governments pressurized by enlargement-opposing industries are free to utilize AD measures for their protection irrespectively if they are seriously harmed by foreign industries of 'like products'. Whether industries receive contingent protection against new WTO members hence depends on the degree they feel economically challenged by the candidate's products and if they are afraid of losing the race, independent of the true extent of dumping. Before further evolving these considerations, and before elaborating the logic of the political economy of contingent protection, a few baseline assumptions and framework conditions need to be specified. Please note that these assumptions are not limited to this chapter, but that they are generally applicable to all theoretical considerations within this book.

4.1.1 Assumptions and Theoretical Framework

I first assume that, among the incentives for WTO membership as listed in Chapter 3, the primary motivation to join the WTO is the liberalization of trade in goods and services accompanied by the accession. The objective of the Chinese government was for instance to receive improved market access for exports to other WTO members to further increase international sales of its fast growing industries. The price China pays for improved access to world markets is the reduction of its own trade barriers in the form of tariff concessions and large scale domestic reforms. The reduction of Chinese trade barriers lower other WTO members' market entry costs and improve their sales on Chinese markets. Hence, the primary enlargement motivation of both sides – applicants' as well as old members' governments – consists in the reciprocal exchange of market access (Hillman 1989; Yarbrough and Yarbrough 1986). The accession of new members consequentially triggers a step towards free-trade for varying industries of exporting WTO members.[9]

Second, as known from numerous approaches in the political economy of trade and protection (e.g. Grossman and Helpman 1994; Hillman 1989; Magee et al. 1989; Mayer 1984), trade liberalization generates winners and losers among domestic societal groups, which can be summarized as follows. Easing market

---

[9] Reciprocal trade liberalization between WTO members and applicant countries is not necessarily symmetric, that is, individual governments are likely to demand more market access than they are willing to give (Rhodes 1989). The product of the time-consuming bilateral market access negotiations is the candidate's tariff schedule, which forms the basis for future trade relations.

access for foreign imports generates competition stress for domestically sold products, which negatively affects the incomes of factors of production specific to these industries. Industry-specific employees and workers of import-competing corporations will oppose a trade liberalization affecting their industry. Export-oriented corporations generally profit from domestic price drops and from cutbacks of foreign trade barriers. Exporters are thus the beneficiaries of the negotiated foreign market access through tariff liberalizations. The opening of the Chinese economy along WTO accession negotiations reduced for example the market access costs of other WTO members and increases their exporters' sales – especially in combination with the Chinese demand for varying goods.[10] Last but not least, consumers profit from the multilateral trade liberalization in the course of a new member's WTO accession. The elimination of tariff and quota rents for import-competing industries and the import of foreign goods lower domestic prices and increases product diversity.

This broad-based interest typology and the antecedent assumptions form the basis for the theoretical explanation of contingent protection against candidate WTO members in general and against China in particular. Knowing about the redistributive welfare effects of trade liberalization with China for the respective interests among their electorate, vote-maximizing WTO governments face the political-support trade-off between winners and losers of China's accession. If the affected industry consists of large and labour-intensive corporations, not offering protection will cost governments the votes of workers and employees employed in that industry. However, if governments act on behalf of protectionist special interests and labour-owners of the affected industry by opposing enlargement, they risk losing political support from China-directed exporters and votes from free-trade oriented consumers. Contingent protection offers an efficient solution for WTO member governments confronted with such contradicting trade-policy interests for three broad reasons.

First, contingent protection solves the domestic interest group trade off: Governments can support WTO enlargement including the necessary liberalization steps, while simultaneously protecting special industries through AD measures.

---

[10] An exception to the general wisdom that exporters profit from trade liberalization is the case in which a powerful new member such as China also increases competition for exporters on third markets. More, specifically 'third-market competition' emerges when export-oriented corporations of the new member receive equal access to foreign markets primarily dominated by identical goods from established WTO exporters.

The nature of AD allows for focused protectionism, sharply targeted at specific products and countries. AD filings can be brought forward by actors on behalf of certain industries; decisions are based on the injury determination procedure by national authorities.

Second, and with an equivalent logic, contingent protection solves intra-organizational conflicts between those members opposing accession due to protectionist attitudes and the beneficiaries of the applicant's integration. AD measures are not only industry- but also country specific. They are discriminatory in contrast to tariff policies applied to products from *all* WTO members. The discriminatory nature of AD measures reduces the risk of trade conflicts brought before the WTO dispute settlement body.

Third, AD measures formally do not infringe on the WTO doctrine of non-discrimination. AD rules leave nevertheless sufficient loopholes for their protectionist utilization. Contingent protection hence circumvents legal conflicts. Governments face the simple question why they should infringe on the WTO doctrine of non-discrimination by imposing tariffs and quotas against countries, if this is allowed in disguise of AD. These three broad features render AD measures a superior protectionist tool compared to universal import tariffs. They can hence be considered as primary motives for the application of AD duties also against candidates during their accession to the WTO. The following part illustrates the motives of conducting administered protection against applicants in more detail and mounts into hypothesized determinants for increasing AD measures during the accession process.

4.1.2 Antidumping I: Minimizing Domestic Conflicts

Contingent protection solves domestic interest conflicts between groups favouring WTO enlargement and accompanied trade liberalization and those who oppose it. Vetoing accession or inhibiting trade liberalization in bilateral market access negotiations displeases export-oriented industries and consumers. Granting applicants full market access in the course of accession negotiations upsets on the other hand import-competing industries suffering from the potential influx of cheap goods. Either way, governments of WTO members participating in the accession process lose votes from one side or the other. The application of AD duties on specific imports can satisfy the protectionist demands of import-competitors, without having to pursue general trade-distorting policies offending domestic free-trade interests. Governments hence publicly promote WTO enlargement and conduct trade liberalization for free-trade industries, while giving protectionist import-competitors the possibility of applying for AD measures.

China's booming economy and the accompanied trading power along with simplified market access to other WTO economies challenges for example industries specialized in the production of goods similar to those originating in China. Those who suffer most from the low prices of Chinese manufactures are established import-competing industries within old WTO members who cannot lower their costs of production or do not want to lower prices for rent-seeking motives. In other words, uncompetitive domestic import-competitors are traditionally the most prominent opponents of free-trade moves affecting their industry.[11]

Industries feeling contested by foreign producers file a complaint to national AD authorities stating that given foreign industries, e.g. textiles producers in China, export their products at prices below domestic prices (price dumping) or below costs of production (cost dumping) (Messerlin and Tharakan 1999). Authorities verify the complaint. If they determine dumping practices, if these practices seriously injure the complainant, and if the complaining industry is of a significant size, authorities are free to levy tariffs on imports of 'like products'. Remember that due to the vague nature of AD rules and due to the intransparency (lack of transparency) of national injury determination procedures, neither dumping has to be de facto prevalent nor does it need to seriously harm the complainant to implement AD measures.

Given that applying AD measures are a form of 'administered protection' (Finger et al. 1982), the impact of political pressure and lobbying variables on AD outcomes is difficult to assess. The injury determination procedure, that is, the calculations if AD measures are justified, is conducted by formally independent but often politically appointed institutions. And although these institutions have sufficient leeway to authorize AD measures even if industries are *not* injured by foreign imports, they must follow the institutional rules, which are the outcome of political decision processes. In other words, while politicians cannot impact

---

[11] In chapter 5 I also point to the possibility of exporters denying trade liberalization with China due to their fear of losing market shares abroad. This logic is however analogous to that of import-competition: China's export power lowers the prices on international markets, for which the export competition increases for old WTO Members' industries of like products.

each individual AD decision, they decide how easy it is for national institutions to pave the way for contingent protection (Tharakan 1995).

Moreover, the freer authorities are to grant AD measures, the more they will, simply because administrators try to consolidate their power. "It will be self-destructive for an administrative unit which is set up specifically to investigate dumping complaints to interpret the rules and regulations with a free trade bias. Hence some built-in protectionist predisposition in the national administrative structures established to administer contingent protection is almost inevitable." (Tharakan 1995: 1555). Since there is no external control with respect to national injury determination, the rules of the AD game simply evolve over time according to the national demand for protection (Prusa 2001).

Niels and ten Kate (2004) even report Mexican antidumping cases which have been initiated '*ex officio*', that is, by the antidumping authority itself without formal complaints. This Mexican antidumping wave, initiated in the early 1990s, mounted into a phase of protectionism in which for example 11 per cent of Chinese exports to Mexico have been burdened with antidumping measures (Niels and ten Kate 2004: 979).

Import-competing domestic industries are the ones who profit most from this form of protection. Finger (2002) compares any trade restriction decisions based on injury determination to "… a soccer pitch with only one goal" (Finger, 2002: 203). Successfully complaining import-competitors with successful dumping complaints score, while interest groups bearing the costs of the measures do not. The administrative nature of antidumping regulation inhibits however the inference of a direct causal mechanism between protectionist demands, political pressure and increasing AD duties. Politicians cannot impact AD decisions in the short run, but can change the rules of AD regulations, which increases the probability of successful individual complaints. Export-oriented free-traders oppose protectionism and profit from additional sales to the applicant with its integration into the WTO. Since AD authorities are officially autonomous, governments are hard to blame for increasing administered protection. If at all, domestic free-trade interests can hold governments liable for *not* correcting protectionist bias in AD administrations.

Above all, if governments manage to protect import-competitors with AD measures, there is no need to slow down market access negotiations with WTO candidates for free-trade oriented industries. Special domestic industries receive the protection they demand without having to oppose trade negotiations. Exporters and consumers profit from enlargement and new markets abroad. Even if pro free-traders dislike the increasing number of AD measures levied on imports, they cannot hold national governments accountable due to the administrative nature of the AD decision-making process. Governments hence solve domestic trade-policy conflicts by promoting accession on the one hand, while designing national AD administration as a self-service counter for protection on the other.

4.1.3 Antidumping II: Minimizing Interstate Conflicts

A second line of conflict follows directly from the above sketched domestic interests: WTO member countries dominated by industries which gain from trade liberalization with applicants will strongly promote their accession. Conflicts arise with more reluctant members who slow down the enlargement process to protect special national industries. Again, industry specific AD duties enable originally contra-integrationist governments to protect import-competitors without having to veto enlargement. The silent way of contingent protection enables governments to publicly endorse applicants' WTO accession, to hold on to previously negotiated liberal trade-policies with other WTO members, while simultaneously satisfying the protectionist interests of domestic industries.

In more general terms, the application of AD measures for contingent protection solves intra-organizational conflicts since AD does formally not infringe on the WTO doctrine of non-discrimination. AD rules nevertheless leave sufficient loopholes for their protectionist utilization. Contingent protection hence circumvents legal conflicts. Governments face the simple question why they should infringe on the WTO doctrine of non-discrimination by imposing tariff and quotas, if this is allowed in disguise of AD. At the same time, antidumping- and safeguard rules are of such a vague institutional design and enable national governments to use the measures for the limitation of imports in general, independent of the degree of injury for domestic firms.

With regard to China's accession to the WTO, substituting old fashion protectionism and logjam attitudes by industry specific AD actions solves domestic and intra-organizational interest conflicts. The disproportionate utilization of AD for protectionist purposes is however not beneficial for long-term trade relations with China – the new member. Upon the date of accession, Chinese industries are legitimated to also file complaints on 'unfair' trade practices against old members' exporters. The probability of retaliation should hence not be underestimated.

Blonigen and Bown (2001) as well as Prusa and Skeath (2001) identify for instance retaliation as a strategic motive for AD especially for relatively new users of ADs – mainly developing and newly industrialized economies. New users direct for instance more than half of their filings against WTO members which have previously targeted them (Prusa and Skeath 2001: 15). Blonigen and Bown (2001) find out that the US AD authority even tends to reduce complaints against countries experienced in GATT/WTO trade disputes if they are additionally major US export targets. In other words, the US AD authority spares export partners if they are credible retaliators. Export-oriented WTO members gazing at the fast growing Chinese market must hence consider future consequences of potential Chinese AD retaliation, or, the more AD duties old members levy on Chinese exports prior to the accession, the higher the probability of being a future AD target by Chinese industries and authorities. Countries will be cautious in filing AD duties against China if it constitutes their major export market.

Having clarified old members' incentives to use measures of contingent protection against an applicant such as China during its accession process, the subsequent final theoretical section narrows down these motives to measurable determinants for the magnitude of antidumping against candidates. All in all, it will be hypothesized that protectionist responses are driven by the affected industry's size and structure as well as by the overall relation of losing import-competitors to winning exporters.

4.1.4 Assessing the Magnitude of Protectionist Responses

The previous sections highlighted the motives for AD protection of specific industries against goods from countries applying for WTO accession. Filing ADs prevents or solves distributional conflicts between winners and losers of traditional protectionism. The general motives also hint towards more specific determinants for the magnitude of AD against applicants. AD regulation of most countries prescribes that the complaining industry needs to produce a significant share of total domestic output.[12] A comparison of the production patterns be-

---

[12] In EU AD regulation, for example, "The case will be rejected if there is not enough evidence or if the complainants do not represent at least 25 % of the total EC production of the product in question."

tween WTO members and the candidate should hence shed light on the general degree of competition. If the applying country is a strong producer of products which also dominate economies of other members, the probability of import-competition rises.

In general terms, the more similar the production patterns of two countries, the stronger the incentives of import-competitors to seek protection. The pure existence of production homogeneities does thereby not preclude that one of the two attacks the other with cheap imports. Hence, the import penetration ratio of goods from applicants to old WTO Members rounds off this mechanism. Consequentially, homogenous production structures between candidates and old members respectively coupled with high import penetration ratios increase the demand for AD protection.

Thus, the mechanisms described in the first pair of hypotheses describe whether specific industries are likely to be affected by increasing competition at all. They constitute the first necessary condition for increased AD measures since old members' industries are likely to demand a certain degree of protection *only* if they are afraid of losing the race against candidates' powerful and labour intense industries.

Hypothesis 1:   The probability of protectionist demands by domestic industries increases, ceteris paribus, with industry specific output similarities relative to the corresponding candidate's industry.

Hypothesis 2:   The probability of protectionist demands increases, ceteris paribus, with the industry-specific import-penetration ratio.

But even if considerable demand for AD protection exists, visible in the form of complaints filed to responsible authorities, the transformation into government action is comparably harder. In political economy models of protection, the supply of specific trade-policies is modelled as a function of governmental and institutional settings, assuming that governments have a direct impact on tariff- or non-tariff barriers (Magee et al. 1989; Mansfield and Bush 1995; Mayer 1984; Rodrik 1995; Rogowski 1987).

---

http://europa.eu.int/comm/trade/issues/respectrules/anti_dumping/index_en.htm, last consulted 12. January 2006

First brought up by Rogowski (1987) and partly confirmed by Magee et al. (1989) as well as Mansfield and Bush (1995) is the argument that the degree to which politicians enforce their local industries' interests in parliament depends upon the relative size of their constituency. The smaller electoral districts, the more receptive are delegates to individual interests. Vice versa, local politicians are more insulated from special interests in proportional representative systems with large constituencies. If politicians carry their small constituency's protective demands into the legislative process, it is likely to end up in tariff- or non-tariff protectionist policies, as has also been shown in empirical approaches (Magee et al. 1989; Mansfield and Bush 1995).

Applying this logic to AD protection is difficult: the causal mechanism from local lobbying to AD measures is disrupted by the administrative process of independent authorities. From this perspective, the supply of AD measures can only be a function of electoral systems if politicians translate the local lobbying activities into designing AD authorities with a protectionist bias. Thus, the smaller the average size of constituencies, the more sensitive politicians are to special interests of import-competing industries, and the more they will plead for changing AD regulations to the advantage of these industries.

Industry structure impacts on AD filings are less ambiguous. Under antecedent considerations, the relative size of complaining industries matters in two respects. First, the example of EU AD regulation demonstrates that only producers with a significant output share are entitled to file complaints against 'unfair' trade practices. Given that this is the case for all AD users, the number of AD duties is ex officio a function of relative industry size. Second, the larger and the more labour intense the industry is, the more votes governments can secure from workers and employees by designing AD institutions to the advantage of these industries. If the industry is not only large in size, but also geographically dispersed over many electoral districts, the size factor coincides with the electoral system argument: the more districts an industry can dominate, the higher the probability that policy-makers act on their behalf. This theorizing is also consistent with the finding of Magee et al. (1989) that, in the US, spreaded industries direct their lobbying activities at local representatives, while large concentrated producers tend to directly lobby the White House. Relative size of a given industry is hence a reliable determinant for the magnitude of AD duties against countries applying for WTO membership.

The subsequent second group of hypotheses thus captures the supply-side mechanisms of contingent protection. Structural and institutional characteristics determine whether the protectionist demand is satisfied. With regard to the conflict minimizing considerations, if governments react to protectionist demands, they do so by supporting AD duties. Relative industry size and labour intensity increase the likelihood of successful AD filings as governments try to secure votes from the employed electorate. Moreover, a certain industry size is mandatory for dumping complaints in most national AD regulations. With respect to political impact factors, I theorize that politicians are especially sensitive to protectionist demands in political systems with averagely small electorate districts.

Hypothesis 3:   The larger the relative output of individual industries, the higher the probability, ceteris paribus, of receiving AD protection.

Hypothesis 4:   The more labour intense a respective industry, the higher, ceteris paribus, the probability of receiving AD protection.

Hypothesis 5:   The probability that politicians design AD administration to the advantage of special industries, and hence support AD duties, is inversely related to the average size of electoral districts.

Besides the domestic institutional factors and industry characteristics, potential intra-organizational conflicts also shed light on more determinants for AD application on goods originating in candidate countries. Earlier, I pointed out that retaliation makes up one of the primary motives for filing AD measures, especially by relatively new users which have historically been targeted by industrialized WTO members (Blonigen and Bown 2001; Prusa and Skeath 2001). Many WTO members expect large gains from expanding their exports to the fast growing Chinese market and would not be pleased if China starts antidumping filings against these exports. Thus, Governments expecting large gains for exporters from China's integration into the world trade system must restrict AD regulation to minimize the probability of future retaliation. Countries with low prospective export-shares to China are therefore more likely to extensively utilize AD as a substitute for protection than members extensively exporting to China.

Moreover, Messerlin (2004) observed that the general pattern of antidumping users has changed throughout the 1990s. During the Uruguay Round, AD users have almost exclusively been industrialized countries. But while the share of measures filed by the traditional users Australia, Canada, the European Union and the United States steadily declined up to the year 2002, "…the remaining developing economies, though still small users individually, together doubled their global share of measures in force during the observation period." (Messerlin 2004: 107). As developing countries gain importance in international anti-dumping filings, one must also expect a country's income to be inversely related to the probability of AD measures against candidates over time.

A further determinant for the filing of AD measures is the increasing probability of WTO enlargement during the accession process. Until the day of its final acceptance as a full WTO Member, an applicant remains an outsider to the organization facing relatively high foreign import-tariffs. Other members' import-competing interests are hence naturally protected by its outsider status during the accession process. As long as accession appears to be unrealistic, there is only little demand for extra AD protection. The decisive part for a successful WTO accession process is bilateral market access talks between the applicant, e.g. China, and all interested members respectively.[13] Consequentially, while for instance China's accession was still far ahead prior to bilateral negotiations, it became increasingly realistic in the near future with every bilaterally reached agreement. The finalization of bilateral talks between China, the USA and the EU in 1999 and 2000 respectively (Yang 2000) have for example clearly signalled the nearby accession in 2001. The awareness that regular import tariffs need to be reduced by the time of China's entry caused governments to start the alternative and conflict-avoiding tool of AD protection. The changing state of negotiations over time will therefore positively impact the probability of AD duties, with a special increase of AD measures in the last negotiation phase after the USA and the EU gave the go-ahead for China's accession.

As a consequence the following last two hypotheses contain mechanisms which are mainly driven by time dynamics. AD protection substitutes trade barriers which have been in place due to the candidate's outsider status. On the one

---

[13] See Chapter 3 for a detailed description of the WTO accession process.

hand, the awareness that tariff barriers need to be replaced by this modern form of protection (Prusa 2001) increased with the probability of accession in progressing negotiations. With the conclusion of every additional bilateral agreement, the date of accession comes closer. Likewise, the pressure increases for governments to replace uniform tariffs on the applicant's goods by AD regulation. On the other hand, governments with strong trade relations to the prospective member are also likely to anticipate future developments and the potential for its retaliation past accession. Countries with large export volumes to the candidate, and thus to China in this analysis, are therefore less likely to initiate AD duties than economies not exporting to the People's Republic.

Hypothesis 6:   The probability of AD measures targeted at the candidate increases, ceteris paribus, over time with vanishing opposition against its membership.

Hypothesis 7:   The probability of AD measures applied to the candidate's goods is, ceteris paribus, inversely related to relative exports to the candidate.

The subsequent analysis will provide a closer empirical investigation of the theoretical considerations, which mounted into the above sketched hypotheses. To proceed, the research design will be explained in more detailed fashion in the following section. After the specification of the sample and the variables, panel regression models are estimated to determine if AD measures have indeed been increasingly applied against Chinese products for the expected reasons in the course of accession negotiations.

4.2 Empirical Test: The Impact of China's WTO Accession on Members' AD Practices

Do WTO governments increasingly substitute traditional and overt protectionism against China by the subtle means of antidumping measures in the face of China's rapid economic growth and its future WTO membership? The main theoretical argument why governments behave accordingly is that AD is – due to numerous loopholes – a legal means of protectionism, which satisfies domestic protectionist interests without upsetting free-traders, and without infringing WTO rules. China's accession to the WTO serves thereby as good example how membership benefits, as e.g. foreign tariff reductions, are simultaneously undermined by measures of contingent protection.

This section aims to analyze the major determinants for old WTO members' application of AD measures against Chinese industries during the accession negotiations and thereafter. Consequentially, the dependent variable of the analysis is the number of annually and industry-specific introduced antidumping measures against products originating in China. Before regressing the number of AD measures on the expected explaining variables capturing the mechanisms as laid out in the hypotheses, I first introduce the sample, operationalize the variables, explain the construction of the dataset, conduct descriptive statistics on which basis I justify the model choice.

4.2.1 Sample, Variables and Dataset

The sample consists of 44 WTO member countries, treating the European Union (EU) as a unitary actor as is common practice in WTO negotiations.[14] The sample of the 44 countries results from two selection steps. Starting off from all existing countries, a subset of the 148 current WTO members has been drawn for the simple reason that WTO membership is a prerequisite for filing AD measures. Furthermore, of all WTO members, a subset of 44 governments was interested in negotiating China's membership conditions within the 'Working Party to the Accession of China'. The Working Party (WP) is the central organ for the preparation of WTO accessions as outlined in Chapter 3. Its members have a strong interest and the necessary power to significantly impact accession conditions and membership rights. In other words, WP members are the core negotiators with a high probability of trying to alter membership conditions through contingent protection if they fail to do so in bilateral market access negotiations prior to accession.[15]

Moreover, about half of the WP members have levied AD duties on Chinese goods at least once during accession negotiations. Hence, all new as well as traditional users of AD protection are WP members. AD measures as well as the

---

[14] See Appendix, Table 8.4 for a complete list of sample countries.
[15] See Chapter 3 for a closer description of the Working Party's composition.

main explanatory factors are industry specific on the basis of internationally harmonized ISIC Rev. 3 production categories. The level of aggregation is ISIC 2-digit, which means that each country's production output is differentiated into 24 individual industries. Trade values, that is, imports and exports, usually standardized by SITC categories have equivalently been transformed into ISIC values. As a result, the sample consists of 24 manufacture industries for each of the 44 WP members respectively.

The timeframe of analysis covers 10 years, which have been pooled to 4 periods. Independent variables of the first period, named *GATT*, cover the years 1993 and 1994, capturing impact factors prior to the WTO foundation in 1995. The second period, termed *Early Negotiation Phase* captures effects of the years 1995 to 1997, when China and WP members slowly started bilateral talks. The third period ranges from 1998 to 2000 and accounts for the *Final Negotiation Phase*. Within this timeframe, important negotiators such as the USA and the EU concluded bilateral talks with China, after which the probability of a nearby accession date increased. Finally, independent variables of the last period cover the years 2001 – the year of accession – and 2002, hence accounting for the *Post Accession Effect*.

The dependent variable – number of AD measures on goods from China – has been counted on an annual basis and summed for each period. The first period additionally contains AD measures which have been initiated prior to 1993, but are still valid in 2001. The last period includes the sum of AD measures up to 2003.[16] In general terms, this ten year period covers the crucial part of China's WTO accession, although the application for GATT membership was already submitted in 1986. However, the credibility gap caused by China's unwillingness for domestic reforms and the Beijing Massacre of 1989 rendered serious accession negotiations and the prospects of becoming a founding WTO member impossible (Yang, 2000). Serious negotiations started in 1995, which is why timeframe of 1995 – 2003 is the one of most interest, with the GATT period as point of reference. In sum, the sample adds up to 44 countries with 24 individual

---

[16] While reliable data for the independent variable has only been available from 1993 to 2002, few AD measures were already introduced against China during the GATT prior to 1993. Neglecting these measures would lead to an underestimation of AD practices against China in times of GATT. While for the last period data for explanatory factors has only been available for the years 2001 and 2002, AD measures initiated in 2003 have additionally been included to achieve a three-year period equivalent to the negotiation periods.

industries over 4 time periods. Table 4.1 summarizes the main variables, their operationalization and expected effects.

Table 4.1 Variable Operationalization and Expected Effects

Variable	Operationalization	Exp. Effect
Antidumping	Number of AD duties levied on products originating in China by date of initiation, still in place by 2001 or initiated thereafter.	/
Main Variables		
Industry Similarity	Spearman Rank Correlation Coefficient (Rho). Measures production similarity within each 2-Digit ISIC Industry between China and the sample countries, respectively.	+
Industry Dependency	Log of 2-Digit ISIC industry output divided by Log of GDP	+
Import Penetration Ratio	Log of Imports from China (converted from SITC to ISIC) divided by Log of 2-Digit ISIC industry output	+
Export Share	Log of 2-Digit ISIC exports to China (converted from SITC to ISIC) divided by Log of 2-Digit ISIC industry output	-
Controls		
GDP Per Capita	GDP Per Capita	+/-
District Magnitude	Total lowest tier seats divided by number of electoral districts	-
GATT	1993 – 1994 plus prior AD measures; annual values pooled (mean); AD measures summed; period of reference	/
Early Negotiations	1995 – 1997	+
Final Negotiations	1998 – 2000	+
Post Accession	2001 – 2002 plus AD measures from 2003	+
Industry Dummies	24 ISIC 2-Digit Industries; expected effect for labour intensive industries	+

Analogous to the hypothesized impacts on the probability of AD filings against China, the industry-specific variables of main interest are *industry similarity*, *industry dependency*, the *import penetration ratio* and *export shares to China*. The aggregated variable *district magnitude* serves to control for the impact of the electoral system and *GDP per capita* keeps track of income effects. The period dummies *early negotiation, final negotiation* and *post accession* capture time dynamics. Industry dummies control for influential industries, providing the necessary information on e.g. labour intensity of producers affected most by AD measures. Furthermore, 44 additional country dummies allow us to control for all unit effects, which is necessary for the estimation of panel fixed effects regression models.

Antidumping measures – the dependent variable – have been collected from the WTO's semi-annual Reports of Antidumping from the years 2001 and 2003 for all available countries, which include industry-specific information on active antidumping measures with their date of initialization. As this is a pure count variable, it does not include any qualitative information on e.g. the detailed dumping margins. AD measures are 2-Digit industry specific, that is, several products can be hit by AD duties within one industry category. The total number of ADs on Chinese goods has steadily increased from 1993 to 2002.

Industry similarity captures the magnitude of competition among individual industries of WTO members and China. The more similar industries are relative to the Chinese industry with respect to their output, the more likely they feel challenged. The spearman rank correlation coefficient (rho) captures dyadic similarities between each member and China over ISIC 4-Digit values. Hence, the higher the correlation of a 2-digit industry between two countries over the 4-digit values, the more similar is their output structure.

Industry dependency is measured by the relative size of an industry and corresponds to the hypothesis that large industries are more likely to receive AD protection. For the construction of this ratio, the highly skewed values for GDP and industry specific output have been logarithmized for the sake of linearization. Import- and export values used for the remaining variables have been treated analogously. The expected positive impact on the probability of AD measures is likely to be accompanied by a positive impact of labour intensive industries, which will be inferred from the industry dummies.

The *import penetration ratio* consists of industry specific imports from China relative to the members' industry-specific output. The demand for AD protection and the probability for its supply – that is for successful dumping complaints – increase with high import volumes relative to domestic output.

Export share accounts for the hypothesized fear of retaliation. If particular industries are major exporters to China, governments are expected to retain from supporting AD regulation against China, which is – by the date of accession – itself entitled to file dumping complaints against old WTO members. In analogy to the import penetration ratio, *export share* is constructed as exports to China relative to industry-specific domestic output.

Data sources for the variables vary. GDP and per capita GDP stem from the World Development Indicators (World Bank 2004). District magnitude comes from Golder (2005). Trade data for the main variables are taken from the PC-TAS database (Trade Analysis System for PC) (ITC/UNSD). Domestic industry output is provided by the UNIDO industry statistics database, published in the International Statistical Yearbook 2005. Trade data is commonly classified by the international SITC standard, while industry output is coded in ISIC categories. These standards have been synchronized as follows.

SITC 5-digit industry codes were transformed into ISIC 4-digit production categories according to a concordance table kindly provided by EUROSTAT.[17] Both – production and trade values – have subsequently been aggregated to the ISIC 2-digit level with the result of obtaining 24 industry classifications.[18] Unfortunately, the quality of national and industry-specific ISIC data provided by UNIDO is relatively poor (Yamada 2005). Compared to the sample countries' SITC export values, more than 50% of ISIC output data are missing values. As a solution, the missing output values have been predicted by means of OLS regression on the basis of the existing export values. Export and output values are most naturally correlated. Inferring the missing values from export structures hence seems plausible and the linear model estimation supports this suspicion. Regressing ISIC output on export values delivers a highly significant positive coefficient with a R^2 of 0.42. Stata's imputation routine delivers similar results.

4.2.2 Descriptive Statistics and Model Choice

Table 4.2 depicts descriptive statistics for all variables. *Antidumping* – the dependent variable – deserves thereby special attention. Of the 3676 observations,

---

[17] The concordance table enables the transformation and aggregation of SITC 5-Digit into ISIC 4- and 2-Digit values. I provide the table, which has been used for the synchronization of SITC into ISIC values within this dataset upon request.

[18] See Appendix, Table 8.3 for a list of industries under investigation.

only 165 values are larger than one. In addition to the excess zeroes, the standard deviation of 6.5 times the mean and a variance of 0.263 are a strong signs for overdispersion. Observations of the remaining variables partly vary, but are generally reduced by those observations, for which the import values are zero. The probability of obtaining AD outcomes for these observations is naturally zero since the existence of imports is the minimal requirement for AD duties. The relatively small number of observations for *export share* is due to the necessary log transformation; missing values of *district magnitude* is caused by the share of autocracies within the sample.

Table 4.2 Descriptive Statistics

Variable	Obs.	Mean	Std. Dev.	Min.	Max
Antidumping total	3676	0.079	0.513	0	15
Antidumping > 0	165	1.764	1.703	1	15
Industry Similarity	3642	0.292	0.497	-1	1
Import Penetration Ratio	3666	0.417	0.121	0	1.025
Industry Dependency	3666	0.840	0.076	0.316	0.960
District Magnitude	3230	13.779	28.598	1	150
Export Share	2516	0.373	0.132	-0.032	0.784
GDP Per Capita	3676	11.004	8.500	1.550	36.465

The structure of the data, especially that of the dependent variable, narrows down the search for appropriate regression models to negative binomial and their zero-inflated specifications for correct treatment of the excess zeros. Especially the overdispersion in the data with a variance exceeding the mean, negative binomial models are superior to the poisson distribution (Long 2001). For illustration, Figure 4.1 plots the deviations of predicted and observed count values for poisson (PREG), negative binomial (NBREG) and zero inflated negative binomial (ZINB) regressions. Although the range of deviations is considerably small, it appears that the poisson model over-predicts zero outcomes, while under-predicting count values up to 4 AD measures. NBREG and ZINBREG perform equally well, which is why these models are preferred over the poisson distribution in the following quantitative analysis.

Figure 4.1 Model Selection: Predicted vs. Observed Count Outcomes

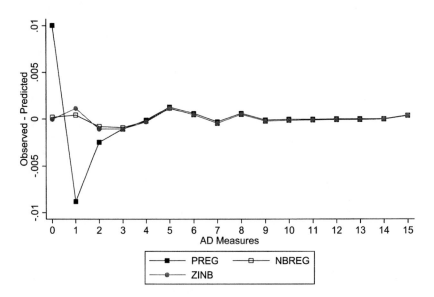

4.2.3 Regression Results

Table 4.3 reports the regression results of the regular negative binomial models, adjusted for panel analysis by unit and period dummies. To account for the panel structure of the dataset with country-industries over four time periods, period dummies capture time dynamics and unit dummies – for industries and countries respectively – control for unit effects. For reasons of clarity, the battery of unit dummies is excluded from the table, but can be found in the Appendix, Table 8.1. One disadvantage of fixed-effects regression models is the fact that the time invariant variable district magnitude cannot be included due to its collinearity with the unit fixed effects. Hence, district magnitude will be estimated in a separate random effects model, whose results can also be found in the Appendix.

The results of the negative binomial panel regression with unit and time dummies are easily summarized: coefficients have the expected sign and are statistically significant – with one exception: *industry similarity*. More specifically, relative industry size and the import penetration ratio of Chinese goods positively impact the probability of industry-specific antidumping measures. AD measures decrease with an industry's export share to China, that is, the more important China is as an export market for old members, the fewer AD measures they file.

Table 4.3 Negative Binomial Panel Regression Results

x Variables (y = AD)	Model 1	Model 2	Model 3	Model 4
Relative Industry Size	9.317***	12.057***	11.712***	7.868***
	(2.849)	(2.772)	(2.667)	(2.038)
Industry Similarity	-0.398	-0.313	-0.235	-0.273
	(0.248)	(0.248)	(0.238)	(0.239)
Import Penetration Ratio	4.345**	5.168**	4.240**	
	(2.027)	(2.012)	(1.914)	
Exports to China	-3.090**	-2.756**		
	(1.302)	(1.286)		
GDP per Capita	-0.239***			
	(0.069)			
Early Negotiations: 1995-1997	0.984***	0.516*	0.523*	0.608**
	(0.346)	(0.305)	(0.294)	(0.293)
Final Negotiations: 1998-2000	2.369***	1.447***	1.391***	1.475***
	(0.416)	(0.291)	(0.275)	(0.273)
Post Accession: 2001-2003	2.528***	1.319***	1.165***	1.305***
	(0.479)	(0.297)	(0.277)	(0.271)
Constant	-15.159***	-18.531***	-18.888***	-13.652***
	(3.421)	(3.315)	(3.191)	(2.133)
Observations	2512	2512	3637	3637
Pseudo R^2	0.354	0.346	0.374	0.371

Note: Figures are ML estimates with standard errors in parentheses, ***, **, and * denote z-statistics at the 99 %, 95 %, and 90 % confidence level, respectively.

The income control variable (GDP per capita) implies that especially new and less wealthy AD users tend to employ duties on imports coming from China. This is also expressed in the results of the unit dummies: Besides the traditional antidumping practitioners such as the EU, the USA or Australia, estimated effects are also strong for Argentina, Brazil, India, South Korea, Mexico and Turkey, using Thailand with low degrees of AD protection as reference.[19] Focusing on the industry dummies it appears that relationships are especially strong for labour intense manufactures of for instance footwear, chemicals, basic and fabricated metals. This complements the fact that not only relatively large industries face a higher probability of receiving AD protection, but also labour intense producers when setting the computer industry as the point of reference.

With respect to the final choice of model specification and the robustness of the results it must be noted that GDP per capita causes a collinearity problem with the time dummies as model 2 demonstrates. Dropping the almost time invariant variable GDP per capita triggers a decline of time dummy coefficients, thereby reducing the level of significance for the early negotiation period to 10 %. By excluding GDP per capita, the remaining models provide robust results, even though the number of observations increases by more than 1000, due to dropping export shares. However, the coefficients for the last two periods (final negotiations and post accession) are in every model specification two to three times larger than for the early period. This supports the theoretical expectation that the hypothesized effects grow stronger with the increasing likelihood of China's accession. Under these considerations and due to the fact that the collinearity effects caused by GDP per capita are unique to the period dummies, model 1 – including all variables – is referred to as the baseline model.

For further analysis and testing of robustness, Table 4.4 contains the results of zero inflated negative binomial models, not only accounting for overdispersion, but also for excess zeros. To control for zero inflation, a second step is added to the maximum likelihood (ML) estimation, which is a binary equation providing ML estimates for the probability of always producing zero outcomes on the dependent variable. In other words, it helps to identify those variables causing excess zeros.

Again, relative industry size is strongly significant, while industry similarity is not. The most notable deviations from earlier results is that both export shares to China as well as the import penetration ratio turn insignificant – at least in the logistic regression. While this also applies to the analysis of zero inflation, the import penetration ratio is robustly significant at the 10% level. The negative coefficient implies that with increasing imports from China relative to domestic

---

[19] Please see the Appendix, Table 8.1 for the full model specification including results of all dummy variables and further technical considerations.

production, the likelihood that non-AD users permanently abstain from applying
ADs falls.

Table 4.4 Zero Inflated Negative Binomial Panel Regression.
Dependent Variable: AD Measures

x-Variables (y=AD)	Model 1	Model 2	Model 3
Relative Industry Size	8.373***	10.809***	10.355***
	(2.834)	(2.774)	(2.722)
Industry Similarity	-0.200	-0.098	-0.154
	(0.270)	(0.269)	(0.241)
Import Penetration Ratio	2.646	3.180	2.309
	(2.179)	(2.194)	(2.170)
Exports to China	-2.091	-1.702	
	(1.486)	(1.505)	
GDP per Capita	-0.224***		
	(0.069)		
Early Negotiations:	0.899***	0.430	0.471
1995-1997	(0.345)	(0.306)	(0.295)
Final Negotiations:	2.210***	1.305***	1.310***
1998-2000	(0.422)	(0.298)	(0.279)
Post Accession:	2.345***	1.165***	1.089***
2001-2003	(0.483)	(0.299)	(0.278)
Constant	-13.758***	-16.672***	-16.610***
	(3.465)	(3.408)	(3.372)
Zero Inflation			
Relative Industry Size	30.081	28.581	25.082
	(19.647)	(18.670)	(20.961)
Industry Similarity	1.762	1.785	
	(1.556)	(1.468)	
Import Penetration Ratio	-29.153*	-28.975*	-29.422*
	(17.178)	(16.133)	(15.585)
Exports to China	-0.652	-0.765	
	4.767	4.796	
Constant	-15.194	-13.817	-10.524
	(14.396)	(13.711)	(15.631)
Observations	2512	2512	3637

Note: Figures are ML estimates with standard errors in parentheses, ***, **, and *
denote z-statistics at the 99 %, 95 %, and 90 % confidence level, respectively.

Hence, while the standard negative binomial model indicates a positive relationship between relative imports and the *number* of ADs, the zero inflated versions suggest a negative relationship between imports and the *absence* of AD practices. While the zero inflated models question the robustness of export shares and import penetration, the results achieved for the time and unit effects are equivalent to earlier models. Effects increase over time and are especially pronounced for labour intensive industries.

Unfortunately, the fixed effects models specified so far cannot account for the time invariant variable *district magnitude* since it perfectly correlates with the unit effects and hence biases the results. To check for its impact, a third battery of models has been estimated by random effects negative binomial regression.[20] *District magnitude* is found to be negatively related to the number of AD measures as theoretically predicted, but not robustly significant over several specifications.

The remaining results are equivalent to the fixed effects models except for *export shares*, which turns significantly positive. These results must be treated cautiously: the unit effects are not distributed randomly, which violates the main assumption of random effects models. Without considering unit effects, a true negative relationship between AD measures and *district magnitude* cannot be inferred.

4.2.4 Predicted Probabilities

In sum, the baseline model of the regular negative binomial fixed effects regression is the most appropriate for further interpretation, but with a cautious treatment of the *export share* variable, which has proven to be insignificant in the zero inflated specifications. I therefore transform the model 1 results of the negative binomial regression to predicted probabilities for the most dominant count values (0 to 4), which account for 99.7% of total count outcomes in the data.

Table 4.5 displays the variables' effects (in %) without differentiating between the time intervals. While values vary from minimum to maximum for the three main variables, values of all other variables are set to their highest impact values. Lower ceteris paribus values, e.g. median values for all variables, always

---

[20] See the Appendix, Table 8.2 for results.

lead to zero outcomes, that is, a constant probability of 100 % for zero outcomes independent of individually changing values. Hence, the effects are considerably small: with all variables set to their maximum (minimum for *export shares*), there is only a 13.6 % probability of achieving one AD measure per country and ISIC 2-Digit industry and only a 2.2 % likelihood for two ADs. Moreover, lowering the most influential variable to its minimum values reduces the probability for one AD duty to 0.1 % – even with all other variables held constant at their maximum impact values.

Table 4.5   Predicted Probabilities of Count Values with Changing Values of Independent Variables

Main Variables	Values	AD Outcome	0	1	2	3	4
Import Penetration	Minimum		99.8	0.2	0.0	0.0	0.0
	Median		98.4	1.6	0.0	0.0	0.0
	Maximum		83.7	13.6	2.2	0.4	0.1
Industry Size	Minimum		99.9	0.1	0.0	0.0	0.0
	Median		93.6	6.0	0.4	0.0	0.0
	Maximum		83.7	13.6	2.2	0.4	0.1
Export Shares	Maximum		98.5	1.5	0.0	0.0	0.0
	Median		94.8	4.9	0.3	0.0	0.0
	Minimum		83.7	13.6	2.2	0.4	0.1

This picture changes when taking into account the varying impact of individual time periods. Figures 4.2 to 4.4 plot predicted probabilities for zero outcomes of AD measures with changing values of the three main variables relative industry size (Figure 4.2), import penetration (Figure 4.3) and export shares (Figure 4.4). Again, the negative binomial model 1 forms the basis for the graphs with all other variables held constant at their maximum level.

As was theoretically expected, effects are less pronounced during the early negotiation phase than in the final negotiation phase and the time past China's accession. The largest overall effect is caused by the relative size of an industry – as can be seen in Figure 4.2. During the last periods, the probability of not filing AD measures drops by nearly 80% as relative industry size approaches its maximum value.

**Figure 4.2   Predicted Probabilities of Zero Outcomes:
Relative Industry Size**

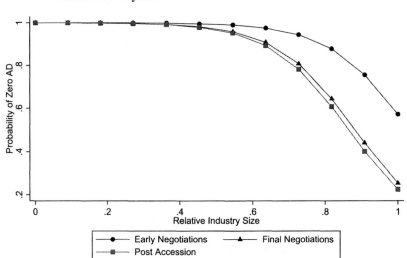

Figure 4.3 depicts a similar impact of the import penetration ratio on the probability of a zero AD outcome. In the early negotiation phase, countries abstained from applying AD measures against China with a 70% probability *despite* high import penetration ratios. During the final negotiation phase and the time past China's accession, the probability that old WTO members refrain from AD practices drops to only 30%, ceteris paribus.

The inverse relationship between the probability of AD filings and exports directed to China is plotted in Figure 4.4. The probability that countries *do not* levy AD duties on products from specific industries increases with the export shares of these industries to China. Again, this relationship representing countries' fear of retaliatory trade policies is stronger in the periods centring on China's accession date, as indicated by the steeper slopes.

**Figure 4.3   Predicted Probabilities of Zero Outcomes:
                     Import Penetration Ratio**

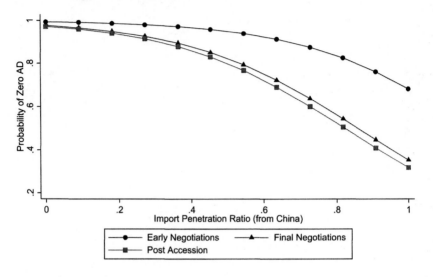

**Figure 4.4   Predicted Probabilities of Zero Outcomes:
                     Export Shares to China**

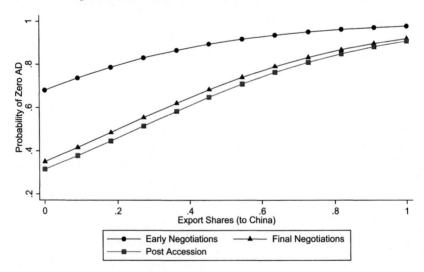

All in all, differentiating the estimated effects into three time intervals reveals their relatively stronger magnitude in China's final negotiations phase and thereafter, compared to early membership ambitions. This perfectly reflects theoretical expectations about protectionist responses growing stronger with an increasing likelihood of China's accession: in the final negotiation phase, the majority of WP members concluded – or had already concluded – bilateral talks with Chinese delegates. Being aware of China's nearby accession, protectionist members have granted special domestic industries larger numbers of AD filings.

Before further interpreting the empirical results in the light of the theory, they can be summarized as follows. The variable having the strongest impact on AD outcomes is the relative size of ISIC 2-Digit industries for all regressions – regardless if negative binomial fixed effects, zero inflated negative binomial fixed effects or random effects models. The import penetration ratio especially affects the probability of zero outcomes. Considering the unit effects, these mechanisms are strongest for labour intensive industries. Time – as a proxy for China's accession probability – plays a crucial role.

Estimated effects increase drastically from the early to the final negotiation phase and remain at this level after China's accession. Mixed results have been reported for export shares. While negatively signed and statistically significant in the main model battery, it remains insignificant in the zero inflated specifications. Hence, export shares as measures for the fear of retaliation do impact the probability of AD measures, but only when treating them in one equation not accounting for zero inflation. No inference can be made for district magnitude: the inclusion of this time invariant variable into the fixed effects models biases the results since it correlates with the unit effects. While the results of random effects models correspond to the theoretical expectation, they are unfortunately not robust. In addition, considering the systematically drawn sample, unit effects are not random, which renders reliable inference impossible.

Last but not least, coefficients for the main variable *industry similarity* are insignificant throughout all model specifications. The first explanation for these results is straightforward: there is no relation between ISIC 2-Digit industry similarities and the number of ADs. However, the second explanation, namely mis-operationalization, must be given some thought. Does the variable really capture output similarities within 2-Digit sectors between China and each WP member?

Industry similarities are captured over the 4-digit subcategories, which vary for instance from 17 more specific categories in the food industry to only 3 in the production of rubber. By using the spearman rank correlation coefficient, similar bivariate structures of these subcategories lead to high variable values for the aggregate 2-Digit industry. However, AD demand might still be higher for similar industries of higher specialization not captured by the 4-Digit level. In other words, output similarities of highly specialized industries do not necessarily lead to higher variable values. Hence, industry similarities in fact do not impact AD duties if measured on the 4-Digit ISIC level. Testing if this is also true for specialized industries requires a comparison of more disaggregated outputs.

The subsequent section now asks what the implications of these results for the theory of protectionist responses to China's WTO accession are. It summarizes all findings, puts them in a theoretical perspective and integrates this Chapter's inference into the broader scope of the entire book.

4.3 Theoretical Implications and Concluding Remarks

During the early accession phase of China to the WTO, it was prevalent for WTO members that China's accelerated growth especially in export sectors coupled with market access liberalization to foreign markets would drastically change the competitive situation at home and on world markets. Given the progressing worldwide reduction of import tariffs, governments knew that if they want to protect domestic industries from Chinese competition in the future without having to veto its membership, they need alternative protection tools such as AD measures. The main argument of this chapter is hence that by designing the administrative process in such a way that it is biased towards positive AD decisions, governments offer a sufficiently large degree of protection to import-competing interests, while still fostering China's accession and trade liberalization to the advantage of other industries' free-traders.

In the tradition of political economy approaches of trade and protection, governments' action in this regard is not arbitrary, but a function of protectionist demands. It is expected for protectionist demands to increase with the level of contestation by foreign industries, and that competition increases with production similarities of these industries. However, the empirical results do not support this first hypothesis, at least not at the low level of disaggregation with similarities computed for ISIC 4-Digit values. Consequentially, AD duties are independent from competition among aggregated and therefore heterogeneous industries. This does not foreclose the possibility that similarities and hence competition of large and specialized industries triggers higher degrees of AD protection. The latter option is – due to a lack of highly disaggregated data – difficult to test for a large sample.

In contrast, the results support the hypothesis that AD duties are a function of imports relative to domestic output of the respective industry. Two mechanisms cause this result. First, industries facing large import volumes from China have a higher demand for protection in general. Second, industry specific imports are a necessary condition to determine injury in the administrative AD process. Hence, with increasing imports the probability that industries are supplied with AD protection does also rise. Relatively large import volumes do therefore foster protectionist demands *and* the probability of their satisfaction through AD regulation at the same time. The level of relative imports does however not determine the magnitude, but merely the pure existence of AD regulation as was indicated in the zero inflated models. This means that once old members are significant importers of Chinese products, they show high probabilities of utilizing AD measures for particular industries. The amount of imports thereby does not impact the degree of restrictions.

The hypothesis that especially relatively large industries – in terms of output – find AD protection is strongly supported by the results. Again, the requirement of most national AD regulations for industries to produce a significant share of the product for which imports they demand AD duties renders this result intuitively logical. But moreover, large industries are also politically powerful and publicly visible. The latter aspect is especially pronounced if size is coupled with labour intensity, as indicated by the dummy variables in the regression models. The more labour intense large import-competing industries are, the more votes governments lose if not granting some form of protection. The analysis further shows that AD only results from very high levels of impact factors. Large and labour intense industries which are truly import-competing are likely to receive contingent protection. This probability drops drastically when only one of the two determinants is reduced– either size or imports.

This is furthermore magnified by old members export levels to China. With China being an important export market, I argue that old members fear future retaliation, since, with its entry to the WTO, China itself is permitted to apply AD rules. And indeed, industries not exporting to China have shown high probabilities of receiving AD duties. Adding minimal export values to the other results over the entire period reduces the probability that these industries will never receive AD protection to 83.7 %, which is still considerably high because it ignores the increasing impact over time. With China's future accession and the need for tariff cuts in the back of their minds, member governments successively introduced AD regulation against Chinese products. The state of the bilateral negotiations within the working party signalled the accession likelihood. With the agreements reached between China, the EU and the USA respectively during the final negotiation phase, accession in the near future became evident. Consequentially, I argue that the mechanisms will especially increase during the final negotiation phase and thereafter, as governments replace China's outsider status with administered protection. The results clearly support this argument. Especially industry size reduces the industry specific probability of not receiving AD protection during the last negotiation period from 100 % to 20 % as it moves from its minimum to maximum value.

To conclude, this analysis supports the overall argument of this Chapter that WTO members did in fact react with administered protection in the form of antidumping to China's accession. Moreover, it has also been shown that this protectionist response is not limited to industrial high-income countries, but that AD is also utilized by less wealthy countries such as Argentina, Brazil, India, South Korea, Mexico and Turkey to restrict the influx of Chinese goods.

This allows governments the balancing act of promoting China's accession with free-trade prospects for exporters, while simultaneously granting focused protection to powerful domestic industries. The concept of 'contingent protection' has almost exclusively been applied to industrial countries as users of antidumping measures in previous research. This chapter hence contributes to this general research strand by focusing on China as a newly industrialized target country.

The results are however even more important for the overall analysis of the distributive conflicts inherent to China's accession to the WTO: not giving industries the possibility to legally receive protection in the form of antidumping measures would automatically magnify negotiation conflicts. Governments pressured by affected industries would have to oppose enlargement to inhibit an increase in import-competition. From the WTO's point of view, relaxing antidumping rules can serve as a backdoor-strategy to make governments, which would otherwise oppose accessions for the sake of import-protection, look at the bright side of enlargement. In sum, this Chapter offers new insights into the subtle form of contingent protection against China – a new and powerful member to the World Trade Organization and it demonstrates that antidumping measures help to reduce conflicts between members and China in its accession process, if these conflicts are driven by concerns of increasing import competition.

However, the empirical analysis has also shown that it is comparably more difficult to detect the detailed mechanisms of why governments and industries react in such a protectionist manner. First, measuring production similarities with output of ISIC 4-digit subject categories seems to be insufficient for capturing the real magnitude of Chinese competition for individual industries. Although similarities for each of the 24 ISIC industries contained in the dataset are measured over 10 to 30 subgroups, this level of aggregation is still high. Antidumping measures are imposed on narrowly defined industries, but categories for the similarity measure might still be too broad for capturing the degree of competition within the special industries.

Second, while most empirical research dealing with contingent protection focuses on one country as a user of antidumping measures, my sample consists of a heterogeneous set of countries utilizing AD. The analysis can therefore not account for special institutional designs of domestic AD regulations. The administrative AD process hence appears as an intervening variable whose impact cannot be controlled for. More precisely, while it is generally assumed that AD administrations act with a protectionist bias, it remains open if government A designs its AD authorities with a larger protectionist bias than government B.

Moreover, the statistical analysis cannot explore to which degree administrations bail out their leeway to file unjustified and protectionist AD rulings. Last but not least, not every AD ruling is put forward for protectionist motives. Some industries might truly suffer from foreign unfair dumping practices. But it lies in the vague nature of the WTO AD rules that a majority of industries and governments utilize them as a general protectionist tool while discrediting those who are truly affected by foreign dumping practices. However, analyzing the micro-mechanisms of AD administration would require in-depth single case designs for each of the sample countries.

In terms of generalizability the analysis is limited since it focuses on China as a single WTO applicant subject to AD rulings. The case of China is special because it is the only new WTO member since 1995, which has – due to its economic power – significantly influenced international markets of manufactured goods. The remaining new members exhibit relatively low trade volumes and they were far easier to integrate than if protectionist responses were necessary.[21]

Although the theory is empirically exclusively observable in the case of China's accession to the WTO, the mechanisms can be expected to hold true in more general terms: To minimize redistributive conflicts arising from increasing competition in multilateral free-trade enlargement, established members must have the possibility of ongoing protection for special and powerful domestic industries. The protectionist bias in AD regulation and the consequential potential for focused protection of import-competing industries hence disburdens negotiation for free-trade agreements.

Thus, one the hand, contingent protection limits new members' benefits from joining because certain trade restrictions such as antidumping measures persist, or even increase past the date of accession. On the other hand, contingent protection can speed up the enlargement process because it minimizes domestic opposition. Powerful WTO applicants, who cause significant redistributive effects for domestic import-competing industries, are hence unlikely to be accepted without the safety valve of contingent protection in the form of WTO antidumping regulation.

The next Chapter follows up on conflicts emerging in WTO accession negotiations in cases where old members do not only try to limit increasing import-competition, but when exporters also feel challenged by applicants on third markets. I argue that multilateral trade liberalization accompanied by WTO enlargement additionally fosters 'third-market competition', which challenges the profits of old members' exporters. While this chapter has shown that governments have tools at hand to protect uncompetitive import-competing industries by e.g. antidumping measures, they can do little against increasing international competition for exporters except for opposing integration.

Governments of economies affected by third-market competition hence strategically delay WTO accession negotiations to prolong tariff and quota rents for ex-

---

[21] See Chapter 3 for a closer description of the accession process and an overview of all new WTO members.

porters on target markets abroad. The explorative case study of China's accession process reveals that the developing and newly industrialized economies affected most by Chinese export competition have indeed been problematic negotiators in the 15 year long bargaining process.

5 REDISTRIBUTIVE CONFLICTS II:
THIRD-MARKET COMPETITION AND THE POLITICS OF STRATEGIC DELAY

The previous chapter identified a strategy of old members to further supply domestic import-competing industries with protection while simultaneously liberalizing trade in favour of free-traders. What has been neglected so far, and what is often also neglected in the political economy literature on trade, is the fact that exporting industries also suffer from increased competition on world markets when trade barriers fall for a powerful exporting nation such as China.

Thus, while antidumping (AD) protection grants a certain degree of protection to import-competitors in the case of WTO enlargement, this does not limit contestation for potentially losing exporters. So far, it was assumed that trade liberalization in the course of WTO accession generates two broad conflicting interests – import-competitors on the one hand and winning exporters and consumers on the other. This chapter adds a second interest group to the losers' side: exporters suffering from increasing competition by the candidate's industries on third markets. Thus, conflicts in accession negotiation arise likewise from increasing export competition.

The antecedent chapter demonstrated that AD regulation is the most efficient tool to prevent competition induced income losses for domestic industries, but that it cannot protect export oriented corporations from increased international competition. This chapter aims to illustrate that member countries tend to delay the accession process if major export sectors compete with potential new members for international market shares, which has largely been neglected in the accession literature.

5.1 Traditional Explanations for Accession Delay

The accession literature at hand highlights the domestic reform reluctance of the *candidate countries* and consequential non-compliance with WTO rules as factors delaying membership rather than analyzing other members' opposition as a function of redistribution effects. In addition to this reform reluctance, accession delay is magnified by excessive demands for membership conditions by mainly the USA and the EU, which "...are using their leverage in accession negotiations to extract commitments from applicant countries that go considerably further than commitments by current members at a similar level of economic development" (Langhammer and Lücke 1999: 839). Hence, conflicts in accession negotiations are exclusively attributed to the major trade powers, while neglecting conflicting issues with similarly endowed competitors or neighbouring transition economies which already managed to enter the organization.

Within this literature, China has attracted by far the most attention among of all other applicant countries. However, the explanations for the 15 year long accession process largely intersect with the above cited general approaches, that is, the home-made deficiencies of reforming China from a centrally planned to a market based economy retarded accession negotiations (Panitchpakdi and Clifford 2002; van der Geest 1998; Wei 1998; Yang 1999). More specifically, Chinese reform measures necessary for WTO accession include "...abolishing all quantitative restrictions on agricultural imports; removing canalization of trade in key commodities; improving market access in the manufacturing and service sectors, according full national treatment to foreign goods and investment, including allowing foreign firms to undertake domestic and foreign trade; and strengthening the protection of intellectual rights." (Yang 1999: 530).

A special obstacle in China's accession process has been the persistence of state enterprises, whose reform is extremely difficult "...as it involves not only liberalization, but often the reconstruction of economic and social institutions such as property rights, housing arrangements, financial and legal systems, and the social security system." (Yang 1999: 518). Chinese insistence on receiving developing country status – ensuring them a number of exceptions from WTO rules – also displeased its trading partners (Lardy 2002: 65).

The delaying role of industrial nations as pointed out by the general accession literature is, according to more specific approaches, more pronounced in the case of China. Especially the unwillingness of high-income nations to accept compromises in terms of market access decelerated the Chinese WTO membership (Langhammer and Lücke 1999; Yang 1999). Unfortunately, the few approaches pointing to other countries' delay intentions are narratives that lack a more analytical account of the motives behind anti-Chinese attitudes in the accession process.

Bond, Ching and Lai (2003) offer a fruitful exception to the purely descriptive analyses of China accession process. In a sequential cooperative Nash bargaining model between three countries they analyze the split surplus of China's accession negotiations when the most favoured nation (MFN) clause is in place. Applying MFN to China was disputed: The Chinese government wanted for example to enter the WTO as a developing country, which would have excluded China from the MFN rule. Acceding to the WTO under MFN meant that the market access Chinas grants to any country in the negotiations applies to every other WTO member alike. Surprisingly, Bond, Ching and Lai (2003) demonstrate that China's relative gains from accession negotiations are larger under MFN since this hardens its bargaining position: Under MFN, "…giving up each dollar to a country means eventually giving up many more dollars to other countries" (Bond et al. 2003: 1). Chinese delegates will thus fight harder not to make excessive concessions in the accession game, which postpones China's membership. This game theoretic analysis of China's accession negotiations is – to my knowledge – the only exception to the above cited empirical narratives.

In sum, when searching for reasons of conflict and delay in recent WTO accession negotiations in general and China's case in particular, one comes across mainly descriptive analyses identifying domestic incapability and reluctance for economic reform as the main accession obstacle. However, this accession literature as well as more general trade liberalization approaches discussed in Chapter 2 neglect a second source of conflict in accession negotiations. The integration of new members into the multilateral trade agreement governed by the WTO also increases the competitive pressure for old members' exporters on third markets. WTO accession negotiations are hence not only delayed by the USA and the European Union trying to protect their domestic markets from the influx of competing goods originating in the accession country, but also by export competitors who fear to lose export shares on third markets through WTO enlargement.

This chapter addresses the consequences of what I dub 'third-market competition', which emerges when export-oriented corporations of the new member receive equal access to foreign markets primarily dominated by identical goods from established WTO exporters. Conflicts arising from third-market competition bear far-reaching implications for the growing WTO. As more and more developing and newly industrialized economies, whose economic growth often depends on only a few exportables, seek entrance to the world trade system, competition increases between them on major world markets. Conflicts in WTO accession negotiations for new members hence increasingly arise because of governments of similarly endowed countries fearing to lose international market shares in exports they heavily depend on.

Limiting negative effects from third-market competition for export sectors is thereby comparably harder than the traditional protection of import-competing industries. While national governments can apply tariff- or non-tariff barriers to restrict domestic market access in favour of import-competing corporations, governments facing increasing competition for their exporters on foreign markets have few possibilities to counteract. In other words, governments cannot directly impact trade relations between the accession country and other WTO members to limit the market access of the new member to old members' target markets. While the previous chapter argued that the optimal solution for the protection of import-competitors is the application of anti-dumping rules, here I argue that the most effective solution to limiting income losses for national exporters is to strategically delay the accession of competing countries. Temporally excluding applicant countries from the trade agreements prolongs quota rents for exporters and gives member governments time for structural adjustments and exporters time to catch up with competitors from the accession country.

The explorative case study of the accession of The People's Republic of China to the WTO in 2001 empirically delineates the logic of strategic delay as a tool to limit negative effects for exporters in addition to traditional explanations. The first half of the GATT accession process was mainly determined by China's slow pace of economic reform. Since the foundation of the WTO in 1995, market access issues between China, the USA and the European Union (EU) dragged on the accession process.

Since 1997, conflicts increasingly emerged between China and competing newly industrialized economies as theoretically predicted. Especially Mexico strategically delayed bilateral negotiations in the face of losing US market shares to Chinese exporters. Other newly industrialized economies with homogenous export structures relative to China additionally demanded trade restrictions for China in the WTO, which limited Chinese membership rights.

Although China is – due to its economic significance – a crucial case for the explanation of the impact of redistributive effects, the logic of third-market competition increasing the demand for trade restrictions and delay is also applicable to other accession negotiations. This chapter hence demonstrates that acceding countries are not only confronted with protectionist and powerful high-income countries unwilling to open up their domestic markets. They additionally face discriminatory demands from similarly endowed and oftentimes neighbouring countries, trying to prevent income losses for export-oriented corporations.

The remainder of this chapter is organized as follows. The next section fills the research gap by explaining the emergence of third-market competition in a three-country example and delineates its impact on governments' preferences and bargaining strategies in bilateral negotiations prior to accession. The explorative case study of section three sketches China's way to the WTO and illustrates that other newly industrialized economies with homogenous export structures have indeed been problematic negotiators in addition to the USA and the EU. Section four concludes.

5.2 Theory: The Impact of Third-Market Competition on the Delay of WTO Enlargement

The following theoretical considerations add a second building block to the explanation of protectionist attitudes towards new WTO members, which has largely been neglected in previous research. It has also been excluded from the previous analysis. Simply speaking, this missing piece is nothing more than a further constraint for national governments in promoting the integration of powerful countries into the world trade system, namely: exporters do not *always* profit from free-trade enlargement with powerful new WTO members such as China.

The previous chapter assumed that governments face the difficult interest group trade- off between import-competitors and free-traders, i.e. export oriented corporations. It has been shown that governments do not have to oppose new accessions if they manage to specifically protect the losers with discriminatory AD measures, without harming the winners. This is correct under the assumption that the export-oriented corporations are indeed a homogenous group of winners. But what are the consequences for the accession process if exporters are fragmented into winners and losers themselves?

What if those interests commonly modelled as free-traders join import-competitors in their lobbying activities against WTO accession simply because exporters of newly industrialized applicants contest their shares on international markets? In other words, if growing export volumes and potential trade liberalization of acceding economies increase the competition for world markets, why should exporters act differently than producers demanding protection of domestic markets?

The first part of the theory focuses on the emergence of what I dub 'third-market competition', which appears if export-oriented corporations from at least two countries compete with each other in the market of a third country. The second part of the upcoming reflections serves to solve the puzzle of governmental reaction to anti-integrationist attitudes on the part of suffering exporters in the case of China's WTO accession.

Administered anti-dumping protection has been shown to be an efficient tool for governments for simultaneously integrating China into the world trade system while still protecting domestic markets from an influx of its products. In contrast, governments can not limit exporters' competition stress by restricting imports. Export subsidies, the only reasonable protective tool in this situation, are inefficient and infringe upon WTO rules. While industrialized countries stick to this trade distortion especially for their agricultural products, it is less common for manufactured goods. For poorer countries, the costs of export subsidies clearly outweigh their effects. Hence, what other option do governments have if a powerful economy applies for WTO membership, but import-competitors *and* a large fraction of exporters prefer its exclusion from the trade club?

The straightforward answer to this question is: veto the accession.[22] While this satisfies the majority of domestic interests, it triggers the next conflict with other pro-integrationist WTO members promoting China's accession. Hence, the second theoretical part argues that vetoing is the best solution for governments facing massive domestic protectionist demands, but that they can not succeed in permanently excluding China from the WTO due to intra-organizational pressures. What results is an accession delay caused by member governments with dominant import- *and* export-competing industries.

---

[22] While this is formally impossible due to a two-thirds majority decision of the WTO members, as long as one of the working party members utters serious concerns about the candidate's membership, the final voting falls through, which grants every working party member de facto veto possibilities.

The argument that competitive threat causes governments of affected WTO members to delay accession negotiations is subsequently evolved in four steps. I first make the baseline assumptions before then secondly explaining in general the emergence of third-market competition with trade liberalization. Third, I contend that export-oriented corporations lobby governments for actions countervailing the rising stress of competition. Fourth, governments strategically delay accession negotiations of the People's Republic of China in the face of domestic pressures from exporting sectors, which is the most effective way of securing quota rents for domestic exporters on third markets. Thus, third-market competition as a source of bargaining conflict needs to be incorporated into explanations of problems arising in multilateral enlargement.

The following assumptions are partly identical with those made in Chapter 4 for the explanation of increasing anti-dumping against prospective new WTO members. These assumptions are supplemented with elements necessary for the explanation of the third interest group: protectionist exporters. Again, the primary motivation of applicant countries in general and China in particular to join the WTO is assumed to be the liberalization of trade in goods and services accompanied by the accession to receive improved access to old members' markets. The price applicants pay are the concessions they make in the form of tariff reductions and trade regime reform, leading to a symmetric or asymmetric exchange of market access with old members (Hillman 1989; Yarbrough and Yarbrough 1986). Two factors of production – capital and labour – are considerably immobile between industries. Factor owners try to maximize their incomes in the short run rather than making long term strategic decisions of changing skills and industries (Hillman 1989).

National electorates consist of industry-specific factor owners. Voters withdraw political support for trade policies, harming their sector and causing individual income losses in the following way: when a respective WTO member government cuts tariffs on imports from China, domestic prices of the given products decrease. Assume that the wage rate of the voters employed in any sector is a function of the prices and the quantities of products sold. Hence, as imports increase, output, prices and the incomes of voters employed in these sectors decrease, for which they will punish the national government with withdrawal of political support for domestic trade liberalization. Factor-owners specific to export-oriented firms profit from bilaterally negotiated foreign tariff cuts. The ease of foreign market access accompanied by tariff reductions increases their outlets abroad and consequentially their individual incomes as well (Hillman 1989).

While this interest typology forms the basis for the explanation of protectionist demands in general, the following considerations highlight that one more interest group can be negatively affected by multilateral enlargement: exporters losing from increasing international competition. So far, exporters have been assumed to be a homogenous group profiting from trade liberalization with new WTO members, but if industry-specific competition increases abroad, exporters lobby national governments for protection analogously to other domestic producers in the face of import-competition.

The example of anti-dumping measures on imports from China has shown that governments are capable of restricting domestic market access despite the accession of new members. However, limiting the stress of competition for exporters is comparably more difficult because world markets are out of reach for national trade policy makers. Before arguing that if governments tend to delay accessions of new members since this is the only way to secure tariff barriers for competitors abroad, the following section elaborates on the general emergence of third-market competition in more detail.

5.2.1 Third-Market Competition: Origins

The newly industrialized and transition economies which have acceded to the WTO after its foundation in 1995 and those whose accessions are underway especially profit from WTO membership if equipped with at least a few competitive export industries. Export-oriented corporations derive large fractions of their turnover from sales in foreign markets, markets in which they compete with corporations from other countries and regions. The competitiveness of exporters partly depends on the costs they bear by entering external markets, that is, tariffs governments levy on imports.

Within the WTO, market access conditions equally apply to identical sectors of all member states. Hence, export-oriented corporations located in WTO member countries face equal foreign market access costs in markets of other WTO members. Tariff rates for exporters of non-member countries are generally higher – if not otherwise bilaterally negotiated. With respect to market access costs, export-oriented corporations conducting trade within the WTO hence have a competitive advantage vis-à-vis non-members. Trade liberalization of competing sectors in the wake of WTO accession eliminates the competitive advantage arising from lower tariff rates. In other words, export-oriented corporations and sectors of a country acceding to the WTO profit from a reduction of trade barriers.

Equalization of market access for economically powerful export-sectors of new WTO members can thus significantly increase the competitive pressure within third markets. Those applicant economies profiting most from WTO membership are consequentially those who cause the most trouble on international markets. This trouble in the form of third-market effects increases with the number of countries participating in the trade agreement and the number of strong export industries. The complexity in WTO accessions is especially large because every member negotiating membership conditions with the applicant on bilateral basis must consider the effects tariff reductions have on its own as well as on other members' trade relations. However, a three country example is already fully sufficient to explain the mechanisms, but first reconsider what happens in the main phase of the accession process.[23]

In the WTO accession process, trade liberalization measures with new acceding members are sequential bilateral. Every interested old member negotiates market access conditions with the acceding country on a reciprocal basis. Domestic export-oriented corporations benefit from increased access to the candidate's economy reached in every negotiation dyad. Third-market competition emerges with the multilateralization of the bilaterally reached agreement: Market access conditions granted to exporters of the candidate country by one WTO member increases the competition for established exporters of another member.

As a result, exporters are fractionalized into winners from bilaterally achieved foreign market access, and losers if the new member's exporters from identical sectors achieve equal access to their target markets in *other* bilateral agreements. If governments strive for exports in trade negotiations accompanied by WTO accession, they must take into account how competing bilateral agreements might hurt their exporters in third markets.

For a better understanding consider a scenario with three countries A, M_{PC} and M_{Shirt}, whereas A is the applicant country applying for WTO membership while M_{PC} and M_{Shirt} are member countries with established mutual trade relations (see Figure 5.1). The economy of M_{PC} is dominated by an export-oriented sector con-

---

[23] Please see Chapter 3 for a detailed description of accession mechanisms.

sisting of corporations specialized in the production of personal computers, while M_{Shirt} is dominated by export-oriented t-shirt producers. Both are WTO members and have reciprocally liberalized market access for these industries since the early GATT times. The applicant A, also a powerful exporter of t-shirts, also heads towards free-trade. A's ambition is to also profit from improved market access to the two members' economies.

Figure 5.1   Emergence of Third-Market Competition

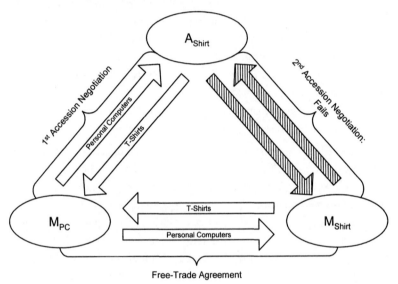

Free-Trade Agreement

Assume that A starts bilateral negotiations with M_{PC} making large scale concessions in the form of domestic tariff reductions for personal computers. Knowing of its weak bargaining position as a newcomer to long established trade relations, A only demands marginal foreign tariff reductions for its t-shirt producers to M_{PC} in return. Understanding that this is a good deal for its free-trade oriented exporters, M_{PC} agrees to this asymmetric bilateral liberalization and supports A's accession to the trade club.

Bilaterally, this is a win-win situation from exporters' point of view. Multilaterally however, t-shirt companies of the other member M_{Shirt} now enter into increased competition with A's t-shirt exports in the third-market of M_{PC}. Established but uncompetitive t-shirt producers of M_{Shirt} potentially lose market shares to producers of A, who profit from the tariff drops in the market of M_{PC}. Hence, M_{PC}'s invitation for A to join the trade agreement diminishes benefits of the T-shirt producers of its principal supplier M_{Shirt}.

However, the rules of the accession game prescribe a second bilateral agreement between A and the T-shirt producing country M_{Shirt}. Since A's accession would exclusively cause costs for M_{Shirt} in the form of third-market competition, there is no reason why the government of M_{Shirt} should conduct bilateral talks with the applicant in order to speed up its trade integration. Note that the emergence of export-competition is a general phenomenon of multilateral moves to free-trade. Its consequences for the accession process of new members to the WTO depend thereby on its magnitude, that is, on the export-power and specialization of the candidate. Among all newly industrialized, transition and developing economies which have acceded to the WTO since 1995, the People's Republic of China has by far the most powerful economy, which is suited best for an illustration of the subsequently explained impact of export-competition on WTO accession negotiations.

5.2.2 Third-Market Competition: Consequences for China's Accession Negotiations

China was expected to largely benefit from its WTO membership with improved market access for its increasing export volumes of manufactured goods. Simultaneously, the logic of third-market competition in multilateral enlargement implies that conflicts in accession negotiations increase with the applicant's trade power and diversity. The crux for China acceding to the WTO is hence that the more it would profit from membership, the higher is the likelihood of other members' competitors being adversely affected on third-markets, which is why they oppose its membership. In other words: the more applicants export, the more difficult it is to join the WTO trade club.

Consider the following stylized real world example for the impact of competitive effects on accession conflicts, displayed in Figure 5.2. Germany and Turkey are both WTO members with established trade relations. China aims to enter the organization and needs to negotiate market access issues with both members beforehand. In the year 2001, the date of China's accession to the WTO, Germany exported air-conditioners for $7 million to Turkey from which it imported underwear valuing $44 million. Both countries are – to varying degrees – exporters of transport vehicles such as railway trains. China is also an exporter of underwear and air conditioning systems to both of the countries. Relatively higher market entry costs compared to the members Turkey and Germany prior to accession create a disadvantage vis-à-vis its competitors.

Figure 5.2   Third-Market Competition and Accession Negotiations

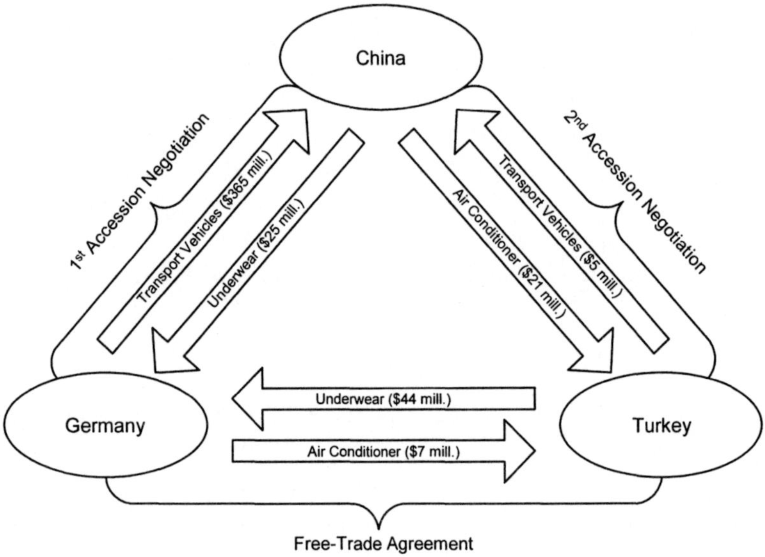

For WTO membership, China has to reach bilateral agreements about future trade relations with both members – Turkey as well as Germany represented by the EU. Assume that the Chinese government negotiates with Turkish delegates first. Both could benefit from reciprocal trade liberalization of e.g. passenger transport vehicles from Turkey to China and for air-conditioning systems from China to Turkey. The Turkish government knows that China is the fastest growing exporter for textiles and clothing with a trade volume of $25 million (US) of underwear to Germany before even being a member. Turkish textile producers would come under significant Chinese attack on European markets as soon as tariffs drop for these products. Turkish vehicle exporters could on the other hand profit from easier access to China, but its accession would automatically cause equal market access to the Chinese economy for vehicle producers from Germany.

Thus, from the bilateral point of view Turkey could benefit from supporting China's integration, but considering this example's third-market effects, Turkey loses twofold when China enters the agreement: Firstly, the previously negotiated market access for transport vehicles is of no use due to the tremendous competition from Germany. Secondly and more severely, Turkish underwear exporters will have difficulties competing with the fast growing Chinese clothing industry as soon as their preferential market access to Germany is eliminated.

Admittedly, this scenario is highly stylized and restricted to only three goods. It nevertheless captures the problems inherent to the WTO accession procedure: Negotiations are mainly bilateral in process, but multilateral in effect. In this three-country, three-good example the Turkish government can quickly get a general idea of causal WTO enlargement effects for domestic industries – regardless whether import- or export-competing – and act accordingly. In reality, the bilaterally negotiated tariff schedules contain hundreds of items and numerous WTO members compete for international market shares of these goods. The number of members conducting bilateral market access talks with the applicant and its export diversity hence exponentiate the third-market competition arising with China's WTO membership.

Consequentially, old member states' exporters will not homogeneously win from WTO free-trade enlargement when new important members join the WTO. In the aggregate, member economies with export structures and targets similar to the applicant will face the highest overall competition, that is, countries that share similarities in their factor endowments. In the case of China's accession this means that especially equally endowed newly industrialized and transition economies are likely to be affected most by increasing third-market competition. This is crucial since it implies that China faced not only opposition from high income countries trying to protect domestic markets, but also from its own ranks if similarly structured economies fear increasing competition abroad. How does this impact the behaviour of affected old members' governments in the accession process?

In the previous chapter I have shown that it is comparably easy for governments to protect domestic import-competing industries from the impact of China's

WTO accession. Does this also hold for limiting third-market competition to the advantage of otherwise losing exporters? I will subsequently argue that this is not the case. Compared to protection of import-competing interests, governments are considerably powerless when exporters lose market shares, simply because that happens abroad. There is – except for inefficient export subsidies – no tool to regulate market forces in other countries. Governments can however preliminarily secure quota rents for their exporters abroad by vetoing accession, thereby extending candidates' outsider status. Before explaining how governments manage to delay accession negotiations, the next section shortly explains when they do it: Governments tend to delay accession if large fractions of their exporting industries suffer from third-market competition, which can not be compensated through new market access of other exporters.

5.2.3 Political Preference Formation

Emerging third-market competition challenges market shares of established exporters on foreign markets as export-oriented corporations from new member countries receive equal access conditions to member economies. With increasing competition the prices of the affected goods decrease and factor owners specific to uncompetitive export-oriented corporations face income losses. The presence of third-market competition thus induces domestic exporters to lobby their governments for actions limiting the negative effects of WTO enlargement. They hence act in the same way as import-competing sectors react to losses caused by increasing import-penetration.[24] This does not automatically mean that governments react to the demand of individual exporters losing from third-market competition.

In general terms, governments will – if at all – only react to these demands if export-competing industries outweigh those exporters which will largely profit from trade with the applicant. Governments will not oppose or delay the acces-

---

[24] As commonly explored in political economy models of protection, the mechanisms of governmental reaction to trade distorting demands vary: while demand side scholars analyze tariffs and protectionist policies as a function of direct lobbying activities (Feenstra and Bhagwati 1982; Findlay and Wellisz 1982) or of the popular electorate (Conybeare 1991), purely supply side oriented approaches treat lobbying mechanisms as a black box and focus on governmental reaction (Hillman 1989; Van Long and Vousden 1991). More comprehensive models reveal crucial mechanisms on both sides: financial and political contributions as lobbying tools on the one hand, and governments' reaction on the other (Grossman and Helpman 1994; Magee et al. 1989; Mayer 1984).

sion process if exporters' direct profits from enlargement exceed others export-ers' losses from emerging third-market competition, not even with powerful domestic import-competitors. As Chapter 4 demonstrates, the latter interest group can be satisfied with administered protection without having to oppose the accession process. Moreover, governments will not veto the accession if no en-tire industry is negatively affected by third-market competition. Single exporters naturally face competition on international markets without and there is no need for governmental action in individual cases, at least not in the drastic form of denying accession to new WTO members. But if the production costs for the candidate's exporters are significantly lower, as is the case for a number of Chi-nese industries, and if entire old members' industries can only compete due to their quota rents, governments are expected to oppose the accession. This does also imply that individual corporations' lobbying activities might mount into subsidies, but not into a veto against new members unless the entire industry is affected.

Further, the relative size of the affected industry plays a crucial role for govern-mental reaction in the accession process. The larger an export industry, the more it weighs for the welfare of the entire economy. The more a country economi-cally depends on an export-oriented industry suffering from increased third-market competition, the more governments will be inclined to limit negative ef-fects arising for factor owners specific to this sector. Take for instance again the example of textiles and clothing, one of the internationally most contested indus-tries. For many newly industrialized and developing countries, this industry con-stitutes besides agricultural products the lion's share of their GDP. If the interna-tional textiles and clothing industry comes under attack from new WTO mem-bers such as China, governments of these countries will be comparably more concerned about national welfare than, ceteris paribus, governments of countries with a second pillar such as the steel industry.

In sum, when negotiating the accession of China to the multilateral agreement, governments need to account for threefold interests: exporters favouring recip-rocal liberalization and the accompanied foreign market access, import-competitors opposing domestic tariff cuts and increased import-penetration, and exporters opposing multilateral liberalization due to third-market competition. However, protectionist demands from suffering export industries confront na-tional governments with a far-reaching problem. Income losses are caused through competition on *foreign* markets, which national governments cannot influence. In contrast, import-competition emerges at home, which enables governments to protect affected industries with specific trade barriers. I subsequently argue that governments facing protectionist demands from large fractions of their exporting industries due to emerging third-market competition need to follow special strategies in the accession negotiations to maximize political support. More specifically, affected governments delay the accession process, thereby prolonging quota rents for national exporters on third-markets, as explained in the following in more detail.

5.2.4 The Politics of Strategic Delay

The previous sections have clarified the emergence of third-market competition from WTO enlargement and the conditions under which governments react to it. Firstly, export competition emerges from the multilateralization of bilateral trade liberalization negotiations. Secondly, governments will counteract if the fraction of exporting industries losing from the increasing competition is larger than the fraction of exporters gaining form the integration of new members to the WTO. The following part will now focus on the question of how governments can counteract increasing contestation on third-markets in the case of China's WTO accession. The argument is straightforward: If the stress of competition is caused by improving trade conditions for China with its WTO accession, the only solution for individual governments is keeping it out of the organization. The problem for governments is their restricted regulative impact on foreign markets.

Contrary to import regulation, the magnitude of competitive effects abroad is not directly negotiable. Especially governments of economies with similar export structures compared to the applicant are hence expected to block the accession process since this is the only possibility to prolong quota rents for their own exporters. I will hence first explain how single governments manage to practically block WTO enlargement despite the fact that officially a positive two-thirds majority of the WTO members is sufficient for enlargement decisions. Second, this accession delay triggers conflicts with those members who have gains at stake from free-trade enlargement, that is, accession delay is limited by intra-organizational pressures and is therefore finite. Single governments can hence protract the accession process, which supplies their uncompetitive export industries with time for structural adjustments, but they fail in permanently excluding China from the organization.

Recall the main phase of the WTO accession process: the core negotiators – aiming to influence China's membership conditions one way or the other – form the working party (WP). While the WP examines the foreign trade regime and the terms of accession in general, each interested WP member is invited to conduct bilateral market access negotiations with Chinese delegates. When all bilateral agreements among the members which have filed the petition for negotiation and the candidate are concluded, they are multilateralized in a tariff schedule.

Acceding to the WTO is impossible before this schedule has been submitted to the WP, which then drafts an accession protocol submitted to the General Council and the Ministerial Conference. From this point on, a two-thirds majority of members favouring accession is sufficient to integrate the candidate into the WTO. Single anti-integrationist governments opposing the accession must hence act earlier in the bilateral negotiations phase. Delaying bilateral talks automatically postpones China's entry date, for which accession delay is potentially feasible for each WTO member government which realizes the negative consequences of enlargement for exporters early enough.

To understand how delay occurs in detail, assume that bilateral market access talks happen in the form of a sequential bargaining game with alternating offers. Generally, one negotiator offers tariff reductions to the other, who can either accept or reject. In the case of acceptance, the game ends. Otherwise, the second negotiator makes a counteroffer containing his/her mutual claims, which can in return be accepted or rejected by the initial actor, and so forth. In standard games of alternating offers a common discount factor accounts for an immediate agreement after the first round since actors are aware of their losses with further time wasted. However, this is only valid if both negotiators have at least some gains at stake and aim at reaching an agreement.

The intention of governments delaying accession negotiations is in contrast *not* to reach an agreement while keeping the bargaining game going, since this is the only way of blocking accession. Hence, the candidate government – in this case China – makes the first offer in the form of certain tariff concessions, which anti-integrationist governments will reject with an counteroffer in the form of excessive demands for concessions, with only few own tariff reductions.

In other words, governments with delay strategies respond to every offer with an unrealistic counteroffer which Chinese delegates will not accept in return. To make sure that China does not accept these counteroffers and an agreement is reached, the respective member government hence demands disproportionately large tariff concessions which would, in the case of acceptance, leave no membership benefits to the Chinese economy. The success of delaying the accession process is therefore a question of raising the concession requirements high enough.

From this purely bilateral perspective with only two players, it seems inevitable that the game only ends when the delay government gives in to an agreement. This could be the case if for instance China introduces large scale voluntary export restraints for those industries which threaten to cause third-market competition for member countries. Hence, an agreement is only in reach if China's government revokes the cause for the delay strategy. But since WTO accession is a multilateral process, external factors further limit the delay duration. Most of all, the potential to delay is limited by the simple fact that other member governments have gains at stake from China's accession, thus pushing reluctant governments to finalize negotiations. With the ongoing protraction of negotiations, conflicts do not only increase between reluctant governments and applicant country, but also between members delaying accession and members pushing China's integration.

For illustration reconsider the three country scenario displayed in Figure 5.2, with China negotiating entry into the existing agreement between Turkey and Germany. China's membership would cause third-market competition for Turkey's textiles and clothing exporters on Germany's market. In contrast to Turkey's exporters losing from third-market competition with China's exporters, Germany would benefit from China's and hence faces increasing opportunity costs with every day of accession delay. Turkey – not responding to political pressure from Germany – delays negotiations by demanding disproportionately large concessions from China. However, if Germany urgently wants China to enter the agreement, its government grants Turkey – the principal supplier – preferential market access vis-à-vis China. This way China can enter the agreement without causing increased competition for Turkey's exporter Germany.

In sum, if export competition from enlargement emerges on a market of a country which itself benefits from the accession of China, it can limit arising conflicts and accelerate the accession process by granting preferential access to established trading partners and principal suppliers. Moreover, although delay is finite, it postpones the impact of the competitive threat and hence allows for a domestic structural change to catch up with foreign competitors. Delaying accession is no suitable strategy to permanently exclude competing countries from the WTO, but it supplies domestic industries with the time they need for structural adjustment. Summing up, this logic generates three predictions for emerging conflicts in WTO accession negotiations.

First, in the absence of severe third-market competition, China and members bilaterally negotiate the degree of reciprocal trade liberalization. That is, they negotiate the exchange of market access. Redistributive conflicts arise when individual governments are strongly influenced by import-competing sectors. In this case, they are unwilling to make domestic tariff concessions, while trying to gain foreign access for exporters. This situation can however be solved if governments protect import-competitors with anti-dumping measures, as was demonstrated in Chapter 4.

Second, in the presence of severe third-market competition, governments additionally face domestic pressures from export-oriented sectors. Governments strategically delay accession negotiations to prolong exporters' quota rents and to gain time for structural adjustment, allowing domestic industries to catch-up with competitors from China. In this scenario, other protectionist tools such as export subsidies are suboptimal, since third-market competition does not affect single corporations, but if the candidate country is powerful enough, large entire industries. The costs of subsidizing entire industries over a long period of time hence outweigh their costs. Other forms of protectionism also infringe upon WTO rules and are thus difficult to justify and implement. For governments dominated by industries heavily affected by third-market competition, excluding China from the trade club by delaying bilateral negotiations is the most efficient way of protection for exporters. The magnitude of third-market competition depends on China's and members' respective export structure homogeneities as well as on the economic dependency of countries on the affected sectors. The more a member economy depends on a sector contested by exporters of the applicant country, the more severe is the arising conflict and the longer the consequential protraction.

Third, delay ends and accession can be concluded when China agrees upon the concessions demanded, if other members reduce third-market competition for affected sectors of their principal suppliers by granting them preferential market access, or if affected old members' exporters manage to catch up with the new competitors during the delay period.

The succeeding explorative case study will elaborate whether the general phenomenon of third-market competition has indeed triggered delay strategies of WTO members in accession negotiations with China. Although China's WTO accession has been a crucial case among all new members since 1995, it nevertheless helps to empirically delineate the theoretical considerations for the multilateral effects of the accession of an economically powerful economy. It hence also contributes to the existing WTO accession literature with an explanation of conflict and delay arising as a function of old members' utility losses from increased third-market competition accompanied by integrating powerful new members into the world trade system.

5.3 Case Study: Illustrating Strategic Delay in China's WTO Accession Negotiations

What have been the major issues in China's 15 year long accession process? Above, I argue that some WTO member governments have no choice but to try to exclude China from the WTO to limit otherwise increasing competition for their export industries on third country markets. This results in an intended and significant delay of China's accession. Surprisingly, export-competition as a serious source of conflict has neither gained much attention in the literature on China's WTO accession, nor in more general theories of international trade and protection. Instead, I have shown earlier that the general accession literature is more concerned with China's internal economic reform problems and the resulting difficulties to bring its trade policy in line with WTO rules, coupled with political incidents which have affected the state of negotiations. While these factors need to be controlled for, the focus of the following case study lies on the impact of third-market competition on strategic delay in China's accession negotiations. Or, in other words, have WTO members with more losing than winning export industries from China's membership significantly delayed bilateral accession negotiations?

With respect to the effects of import-competition, the case study directly builds upon the results of Chapter 4: China's accession to the WTO increases import-competition, but this does not induce governments to oppose membership since they can protect domestic industries by filing antidumping measures on Chinese products. Generally speaking, it is assumed that the pure existence of import-competition does not cause governments to delay negotiations since they have other tools at hand for the protection of powerful domestic interests.

Please note that the case study research design does not qualify for rigorously testing the theoretical consideration. Instead, it is more suited to delineate the accession process and illustrate the logic of strategic delay caused by increased export-competition. In addition, although exemplified by the special case of China acceding to the WTO, third-market competition is a general phenomenon of extending multilateral trade agreements. However, its redistributive conse-quences are only observable when powerful traders require multilateral integra-tion.

Take for instance the WTO accession of Cambodia in 2004. It seems likely that uncompetitive textile producers of other least developed and developing coun-tries did not welcome Cambodia as yet another textiles-producing member in the WTO due to competition it exerts on third-markets. This low degree of interna-tional competition will certainly not induce any government to oppose Cambo-dia's accession. Hence, third-market competition exists, that is, exporters do not always win from multilateral liberalization. However, among all WTO acces-sions since 1995, the *effects* of third-market competition are exclusively observ-able in the case of China.

To proceed, I will first review political incidents which also have had a signifi-cant impact on China's accession duration. Thereafter, I focus on the bilateral negotiation timing of 26 working party members, for which information was available in previous research and international press reports.[25] These negotia-tors are then categorized into 'early negotiators', 'halftime negotiators' or 'late negotiators', depending on when they reached agreements with China. I evaluate each country with respect to its export homogeneities *with* China on the one hand, and its exports *to* China on the other.[26]

This reveals if the dominant part of countries' exporters must be expected to win or lose from China's accession. The results show that the last minute negotiators

---

[25] Individual negotiation protocols, which would have been suited much better for tracing negotiations, unfortunately are classified by the WTO and hence not accessible.
[26] The data used stems from the Trade Analysis System for Personal Computers (PC-TAS), published by the International Trade Center (ITC) in cooperation with the United Nations Statistics Division (UNSD).

are countries, which compete with China in more capital intense manufactures, in which China exhibits two-digit growth rates and countries with weak trade relations to China. These newly industrialized countries from different regions have dragged on the accession process when the EU and the USA had already settled all critical issues. The most reluctant country was Mexico, delaying China's accession by almost one year.

5.3.1 Accession, Negotiation Conflicts and Strategic Delay

Reconsider the threefold benefit of China's WTO accession and the resulting motivations to apply for membership in 1986.[27] First, China's accession enhances market access for export-oriented sectors on both sides – China and its main trading partners. Second, WTO accession fosters the development of China towards a rule-based economy. Third, improved trade relations under the auspices of the WTO are likely to positively affect international political relations among China and especially the USA (Yang 2000: 4). So if benefits from accession are so prevalent for both sides, why has the accession process taken so long?

The General Council of the WTO initiated the formation of the obligatory working party (WP) upon China's application for GATT membership in 1986. With some 50 participating members, the working party to the accession of China was the largest since the foundation of the WTO in 1995.[28] The relative size of China's WP compared to other countries' accessions indicates the overwhelming interest of WTO members in influencing membership conditions. Out of 50 WP members, 44 announced their interest to bilaterally negotiate market access issues with China – a number which already gives rise to suspicion of the complexity involved in the negotiation process (Gertler 2003).

Before delving into the trade- and competition related factors of delay, a number of external and politically motivated obstacles must be considered. First, the political unrest caused by the Beijing Massacre of 1989 dampened the willingness of the international community to integrate China into the world trade system at

---

[27] See Chapter 3 for details.

[28] Every interested member is welcome to participate in the WP, whose size varies depending on the accession candidate. While roughly 50 members participated in the negotiation process of China's accession, only 19 tried to affect membership conditions of e.g. Croatia, which acceded in 2000. Altogether, 20 nations joined the WTO after its formation in 1995. For more details on the composition of working parties see Chapter 3 and Kennett et al. (2005).

an early stage of the accession process (Yang 2000: 15). The resulting unpopularity pushed China's ambitions for GATT membership to restore international credibility and to become a founding member of the WTO in 1995. Unable to lock-in domestic political-economic reforms, China failed to join the GATT by 1995, also excluding it from the WTO. Without the ambition of becoming a founding member, China's rush to accede the WTO slowed down. With increased patience in accession talks, Chinese negotiators tried to improve their bargaining strength to avert being forced to make large scale concessions while receiving only little in return (Anderson 1997: 756-757). Moreover, Chinese insistence on receiving developing country status – ensuring them a number of exceptions from WTO rules – especially displeased its trading partners (Lardy 2002: 65).

Second, the accession leading and six year lasting negotiations between the USA and China, which mounted into a bilateral agreement in November 1999, were hampered by a number of policies not at all connected to trade issues, which have been summarized by Fewsmith (1999). China's reluctance to accept Taiwan's independence and the military exercises of 1995 and 1996 to endorse this position significantly reduced the willingness of the US to engage in bilateral WTO talks at an early stage. As US – Chinese military relations calmed down in the subsequent years, the pace of bilateral market access negotiations picked up and in spring of 1999, when the Chinese Premier Zhu Rongji visited the USA, a conclusion of the talks appeared to be in sight. Although China was ready to make substantial concessions, the agreement was not signed during this visit.

To make sure Chinese delegates would not draw back from their concessions, the positions were published in a 17-page document on the website of the United States Trade Representative (USTR). While this was thought to speed up talks, the opposite occurred because most Chinese officials and domestic interest groups had not been informed about the magnitude of concessions their government was willing to make. The publication of the price China has to pay for its WTO membership hence triggered domestic opposition, which is why negotiations again slowed down from the Chinese side. According to Fewsmith (1999: 31), following this incident Jiang Zemin stated in an internal meeting that "...China had waited 13 years to join WTO (GATT) and it can wait another 13 years."

The bombing of the Chinese embassy in Belgrade in May 1999 further aggravated the stalemate. It took another six months until China and the USA finally reached an agreement, substantially resembling the one almost concluded in April and hence delayed by political factors (Fewsmith 1999). Although Sino – US talks were regarded as groundbreaking for China nearby WTO accession, a number of hesitating and largely newly industrialized economies remained in the waiting loop for bilateral talks.

The delay in the first half of the accession process thus occurred due to political incidents and China's reluctance to align its domestic economic system with WTO rules. Accession progress in the late 1990s was additionally affected by the political climate between the USA and China. At the same time, the pace of bilateral agreements picked up and sources for delay increasingly emerged out of bilateral disagreements with respect to trade liberalization and market access matters.

More specifically, in the late 1990s the accession progress was increasingly affected by bilateral conflicts between China and WP members as theoretically predicted. The focus of previous research has thereby mostly been on the Sino-US as well as EU negotiations. Bilateral market access negotiations between China and the USA started in 1993 and lasted for 6 years, negotiations with the EU have been subsequently been concluded in 2000, and both agreements have most certainly had a significant impact on the timing of China's accession as well as on the substantial membership conditions.[29]

It is nevertheless commonly neglected that the majority of the WP members, who were seeking bilateral talks with China, joined in at a late stage of negotiations. At the sixth Session of the Working Party Meeting on China's Accession to the WTO in December 1997, Long Yongtu, Chinese chief negotiator and vice-minister of Foreign Trade and Economic Co-operation, announced that 35 WTO members have started bilateral market access negotiations with China by then. Long Yongtu (1997) further stated that out of these 35 negotiation dyads, 20 were already near conclusion at that point of time. The following part shows that this turned out to be a fallacy: while Chinese delegates were optimistic to conclude bilateral talks and enter the organization, dyadic market access negotiations went on for another five years until the end of 2001.

---

[29] For details see Fewsmith (1999), Lardy (2002), Liang (2002) or Yang (2000).

The countries which first concluded bilateral talks with China in 1997 are the Czech Republic, Hungary, New Zealand, Pakistan, Singapore, Slovakia, South Korea and Turkey, all of which can be considered as newly industrialized countries specialized in the production of low to medium capital intense goods except for New Zealand (Liang, 2002; Beijing Review, November 1999).

In 1999, the four major traders Australia, Canada, Japan and the USA as well as Chile and Indonesia finalized negotiations with Chinese delegates (BBC Monitoring, December 1, 1999). However, this still left more than 20 negotiations dyads unfinished, most of which again consist of newly industrialized, developing and transition economies.

In the spring of 2000, India, Thailand (Bridges Weekly Trade News Digest February 22, 2000), Malaysia (Associated Press Online April 13, 2000) and Poland (BBC Monitoring March 24, 2000) concluded negotiations with China. The EU, Switzerland, Latvia, Costa Rica and Guatemala further dragged on the accession process to the second half of 2000. Mexican delegates were the last ones concluding bilateral talks with China by the end of 2001, finally paving the way for enlargement.

Subsequently, I will discuss individual countries' negotiation durations in more detail, contrasting them with their export structure similarities relative to China. The countries are broadly classified into early negotiators, halftime negotiators and late negotiators delaying accession. For each group, a table summarizes the key facts with respect to their negotiations and export structures. Of central importance to judge if third-market competition is a reason for delay is thereby the relative export similarity to China, the relative volume of exports to China, and the share and growth of the respective country's export industries.

All trade values within this Chapter have been computed from PC-TAS ITC/UNSD 1993-2002 – the Trade Analysis System for Personal Computers, published jointly by the International Trade Center and the United Nations Statistics Division. Shares are computed as the mean annual (1993-2002) sectoral export values relative to the total exports of the respective country.

Export similarity is measured by the spearman rank correlation coefficient (rho) over the revealed comparative advantages (RCA) of 2700 SITC 5-Digit export groups from "Accordions and Similar Instruments" to "Zinc Tubes". The RCA, or Balassa Index (Balassa 1965) is computed as follows:

$$RCA = \frac{x_{ij}}{\sum x_i} \bigg/ \frac{x_{wj}}{\sum x_w}$$

Whereas x_{ij} is the export value of a good j in country i and x_{wj} the corresponding world output w of the good j. Index values exceeding one indicate a comparative advantage. Growth measures the mean annual changes (1993-2002) of the relative export shares, that is, it captures the growth of individual sectors relative to the development of the countries' total exports.

5.3.1.1 Early Negotiators

Despite the ongoing negotiations between the so called Quad countries (EU and Member States, USA, Canada and Japan) and China, the Czech Republic, Hungary, New Zealand, Pakistan, Singapore, Slovakia, South Korea and Turkey have reached early bilateral agreements with China in 1997. Except for the Slovak Republic and New Zealand, these countries have much in common with China regarding their top export industries. Within this group of early negotiators with approximately only one year of dyadic bargaining with China before reaching an agreement, Table 5.1 reveals that Turkey, Pakistan and South Korea are ostensibly the economies with the most similar export structures relative to China with large fractions of their exports being textiles and clothing.

Following the theoretical considerations that economies with large industries being affected by third-market competition from China delay accession, these countries should on the one hand be expected to delay the accession process rather than reaching agreements that early in time. On the other hand, Chinese textiles exports are restricted by the Multifibre Arrangement, which phase-out by 2005 was regulated under the Uruguay Round Agreement on Textiles and Clothing (Hoekmann and Kostecki 2001).

Quotas on Chinese textiles exports limited third-market competition for other textiles and clothing exporters beyond its accession. Governments of South Korea, Pakistan and Turkey could rely on the existing quota regime for textiles and clothing for the protection of their exporters without causing conflicts in the accession process.

Table 5.1   Early Negotiators: 1997

Country (In the order of Agreements reached)	Discriminatory Measures in Accession Protocol	Export Similarity to China (-1 to 1)	Export Shares to China (%)	Top 2 Export Industries	Export Shares (%)	Annual Growth (%)
Hungary	Footwear & Clothing	0.14	0.26	Electrical Machinery & Apparatus	13.38	5.45
				Power-generating Machinery	8.42	116.31
New Zealand	none	0.01	3.56	Meat and Meat Preperations	17.97	-13.41
				Dairy Products & Birds' Eggs	15.57	-8.87
Republic of Korea	none	0.27	11.18	Electrical Machinery & Apparatus	22.12	-10.26
				Textile Yarn & Fabrics	10.62	-15.60
Czech Republic	none	0.15	0.24	Electrical Machinery & Apparatus	10.12	13.60
				Iron & Steel	7.96	-10.05
Slovak Republic	Footwear	0.05	0.11	Iron & Steel	15.08	5.07
				Electrical Machinery & Apparatus	7.55	12.59
Pakistan	none	0.23	2.40	Textile Yarn & Fabrics	57.04	-0.36
				Apparel & Clothing	18.43	-0.48
Turkey	Kitchenware & Footwear	0.23	0.40	Textile Yarn & Fabrics	16.68	2.96
				Apparel & Clothing	16.21	-5.89
Singapore	none	0.15	4.18	Electrical Machinery & Apparatus	34.07	6.34
				Office- & Data-processing Machines	12.09	1.35

Moreover, Turkey and the central and eastern European countries (CEECs) within this group, namely Hungary, the Czech Republic and the Slovak Republic benefit from preferential trade arrangements with their primary export market: the European Union. Consequentially, to lobby major trading partners for Preferential Trade Arrangements – a mechanism probably most pronounced in US-Mexican NAFTA trade relations (Mansfield and Reinhardt 2003) – is for poorer countries, in particular, a suitable strategy for limiting emerging third-market effects with free-trade enlargement. This way, small countries can free-ride on the discriminatory measures demanded by their larger and mostly regional trade partners.

One possibility for discriminating trade from China to the advantage of smaller trading partners is the demand for voluntary export restraints (VERs). The logic remains the same: the EU pressures for instance the Chinese government to 'voluntarily' limit imports of textiles and clothing to grant Turkish exporters market entry advantages. According to Finger (2002: 199): "In many instances the troublesome increase in imports came from countries that had not been the 'principal suppliers' with which the initial concessions had been negotiated. These new exporters were displacing not only domestic production in importing countries but also the exports of the traditional suppliers. A VER with the new, troublesome supplier could thus be viewed as defending the rights of the principal suppliers who had paid for the initial concession".

Today, the successive phasing out of discriminatory trade restrictions on Chinese goods slowly reveals China's entire export power and the increasing competition for developing countries on third markets especially with respect to apparel, textiles and clothing. Analogous to the protection of textiles exporters to the EU, in 2005, when quotas on Chinese textile exports finally are supposed to be eliminated, 15 of the poorest economies started "...lobbying the US Congress for a new scheme that would give them trade preferences to offset the advantages gained by China and India since the lifting of quotas on textiles and apparel" (Financial Times, May 4, 2005). De facto, this means nothing less than lobbying for ongoing discrimination of Chinese products despite its WTO membership.

Developing countries' exporters thus profit from the import restrictions of their target countries on Chinese goods. Turkish exporters of textiles and apparel have for instance little reason to oppose China's accession to the WTO as long as the EU – their main target market – limits the influx of apparel from China. The same logic applies to other textiles exporters to the EU: In 1995 the EU started bilateral trade negotiations with Algeria, Morocco, Turkey and Tunisia. This initiative, labelled the Barcelona Process, mounted into a number of Euro-Mediterranean Association trade agreements (EU 2005a), granting them market access advantages vis-à-vis new WTO members. The same applies to bilateral agreements reached with Eastern European Countries in the preparation of EU

Enlargement. Finally, in 2005, the EU renewed import quotas on textiles from China despite the initial WTO decision to phase out trade restrictions.

According to the EU (2005b), "The agreement reached with China represents a common, broad and forward-looking strategy for dealing with textile imports from China". Besides protecting import-competing textiles manufacturers within the EU, "The agreement also provides a window for adaptation for producers in developing countries whose textiles exports to the EU were being displaced by a surge in imports from China. This is particularly important for textile industries in the EU's Mediterranean neighbours", i.e. Morocco, Turkey and Tunisia.

Despite the fact that these countries have quickly reached agreements with China in the bilateral market access negotiations, they nevertheless demanded large scale concessions from China as stipulated in the accession documents. The "Protocol on the Accession of the People's Republic of China to the WTO" (WTO 2001) contains numerous discriminatory trade restrictions on Chinese products for the time past accession. Members are free to introduce safeguard measures specific to Chinese textiles imports for a period of four years past accession. Safeguard measures on other specified products can further be legally imposed for another 12 years after China's accession (GAO 2002; WTO 2001). The countries which explicitly list the product-specific protectionist measures in the accession protocol are among others Hungary, the Slovak Republic and Turkey. In sum, the majority of the countries discussed here had only little to fear in terms of third-market competition from China. With respect to the trade restrictions demanded by Hungary, Turkey and the Slovak Republic, it is surprising that China agreed upon these terms at such an early stage of negotiations.

It must finally be noted that the case of Singapore contradicts the theoretical predictions: It shares similarities with China in more capital intense exports of electrical machinery and computers and can therefore be expected to face an increase in third-market competition with China's accession. Nevertheless, Singapore paved China's way to the WTO at an early stage. One alternative explanation is that Singaporean exporters of electrical machinery, who are likely to compete with China are highly competitive: Between 1993 and 2002, their industry accounted on average for 34 % of total national exports and grew by more than 6.3 % annually within the same timeframe. Moreover, as a small country Singapore depends on international trade and is – from a holistic point of view – likely to profit from China's accession to the WTO, especially when considering that 4.2 % of national exports go to China. Although competing with China in the export of more capital intensive electrical manufactures, it also heavily depends on China's economic integration.

This first group of countries underlines the necessity of controlling for ceteris paribus conditions in the search for the impact of third-market competition. First, countries whose export similarities with China mainly result from textiles and clothing industries are naturally protected by ongoing trade restrictions under the MFA. Second, countries with a high degree of export similarity and simultaneously large export volumes to China, such as South Korea, face domestic pressures by those exporters winning improved market access from China's accession. China's close trading partners as well as pure textiles and clothing exporters thus have little reason to strategically delay the accession process.

5.3.1.2 Halftime Negotiators

Three of the quad countries – Canada, Japan and the USA – as well as Australia, Chile and Indonesia completed bilateral market access talks with China in 1999. Table 5.2 depicts that with a high degree of export similarity (.29) and modest export volumes to China (4.3 %), Indonesia was on the one hand more reluctant to sign the bilateral agreement. On the other hand, textiles are Indonesia's second largest industry, which is still restricted for Chinese exporters. Hence, the Indonesian government was not in a hurry to conclude agreements, nor had it reason to significantly delay China's membership.

The agreements reached with the three high-income economies in 1999 play a crucial role in the accession process. Endowed with high capital-labour ratios, they are known to be major importers of Chinese goods rather then export-competitors. They have been less concerned with direct export competitive effects but rather with import-restriction on behalf of domestic industries and their principal foreign suppliers, as e.g. Mexico for the USA. If concerned with export-competition, the high-income countries hence grant their principal suppliers preferential access, as has been exemplified by the relationship between Turkey and the European Union.

Table 5.2 Halftime Negotiators: 1999

Country (In the order of Agreements reached)	Discriminatory Measures in Accession Protocol	Export Similarity to China (-1 to 1)	Export Shares to China (%)	Top 2 Export Industries	Export Shares (%)	Annual Growth (%)
Indonesia	none	0.29	4.27	Cork & Wood Manufactures	12.78	-9.77
				Textile Yarn & Fabrics	8.57	-2.81
Australia	none	-0.04	5.59	Coal, Coke & Briquettes	16.28	0.03
				Non-ferrous Metals	10.59	3.11
Japan	none	0.04	6.87	Electrical Machinery & Apparatus	20.46	1.73
				Road Vehicles	10.06	-1.53
Chile	none	-0.01	4.63	Non-ferrous Metals	38.26	-0.36
				Vegetables & Fruit	10.53	-0.74
USA	none	-0.18	2.45	Electrical Machinery & Apparatus	13.38	2.50
				Road Vehicles	7.42	0.05
Canada	none	-0.11	0.90	Road Vehicles	14.77	-1.79
				Non-ferrous Metals	6.22	-2.15

At this point it must be noted that negotiations between China, the USA and the European Union, which signed the agreement in 2000, were not only time consuming because of issues concerning the liberalization of trade in goods. Moreover, the quad countries also bargained for the even more complex implementation of Chinese protection of intellectual property rights and liberalization of trade in services. This especially affected the opening of financial and insurance services, which China tries to protect in the first place due to its lack of competitiveness (Lardy 2002).

The timing of reaching agreements with the quad countries is hence also important for the negotiation process in more general terms. As they can be expected to have more bargaining power than small export-competing nations, smaller countries are likely to wait until the major issues and membership terms have been reached by the high-income nations, especially the USA and the EU. This way, small countries can free-ride on Chinese concessions induced in earlier negotiations. From this perspective, the signing of the Sino-US agreement sets an important threshold in the negotiation process: the remaining WP members should be expected to quickly reach agreements with China after the six year long and burdensome Sino-US negotiations. Negotiations nevertheless continued until the end of 2001.

5.3.1.3 Late Negotiators

Although the Sino-US agreement was signed in 1999, a large fraction of the WP members continued accession negotiations with China. A number of countries within this group share major export sectors with China and would therefore have reasons to drag on off the accession process. India, Thailand, Poland and Malaysia have all individually reached agreements with China in spring of 2000. While India competes with China for international market shares in the textiles and clothing industry, Thailand, Poland and Malaysia will fear losses for their more capital intense industries such as electrical machinery and computers, as indicated in Table 5.3.

For instance, from 1993 to 2002, the share of these industries' exports in total exports has dropped by an annual rate of 20 % respectively in Thailand. India's textiles industry, which on average accounts for 16.4 % of total national exports, has likewise decreased by 12.2 %. In light of such numbers it seems reasonable that these countries try to exclude a powerful exporting nation such as China from the world trade system and India has consequentially expressed major concerns for domestic industries – regardless if import- or export competing. More precisely, Indian officials tried to restrict Chinese membership rights in the WTO for "...more flexibility to take anti-dumping and safeguard measures against Chinese exports." (Financial Times, July 3, 2001).

While the temporizing of these countries can indeed be interpreted as a delay strategy for the protection of export-competing industries, this is comparably more difficult for the majority of the Latin American and Caribbean (LAC) countries which gave China the green light for accession in 2000, namely Argentina, Costa Rica, Ecuador and Guatemala (in the order of agreements reached). Except for Costa Rica, which possesses a relatively large and fast growing industry for computer parts, these countries' agricultural exports have little in common with China's fast growing manufacturing industries.

Table 5.3 Late Negotiators: 2000/2001

Country (In the order of Agreements reached)	Discriminatory Measures in Accession Protocol	Export Similarity to China (-1 to 1)	Export Shares to China (%)	Top 2 Export Industries	Export Shares (%)	Annual Growth (%)
India	none	0.32	2.11	Non-metallic mineral Manufactures	20.07	-14.50
				Textile Yarn & Fabrics	16.42	-12.26
Argentina	Toys, Textiles, Clothing & Footwear	-0.07	3.25	Feeding Stuff for Animals	14.74	5.04
				Fixed Vegetables Fats & Oils	13.27	2.64
Thailand	none	0.28	3.75	Electrical Machinery & Apparatus	13.77	-20.88
				Office- & Data-processing Machines	9.74	-21.97
Poland	Electric Irons & Footwear	0.14	0.41	Furniture & Parts Thereof	7.69	6.13
				Electrical Machinery & Apparatus	7.24	6.44
Malaysia	none	0.14	3.70	Electrical Machinery & Apparatus	28.80	-9.33
				Telecom. & Sound-recording Equipment	15.37	-13.52
EU	Kitchenware & Footwear	-0.17	0.77	Electrical Machinery & Apparatus	9.13	-0.01
				Specialized Machinery	7.54	-3.86
Costa Rica	none	0.01	0.35	Office- & Data-processing Machines	17.34	45.30
				Coffee, Tea, Cocoa & Spices	12.66	-26.00
Ecuador	none	0.05	0.96	Fish & Crustaceans	48.26	-3.20
				Coffee, Tea, Cocoa & Spices	9.27	-5.49
Guatemala	none	0.07	0.03	Coffee, Tea, Cocoa & Spices	30.74	-2.12
				Sugars, Sugars Preparations & Honey	14.42	1.88
Latvia	none	0.05	0.05	Cork & Wood Manufactures	10.61	11.71
				Textile Yarn & Fabrics	9.89	-3.90
Switzerland	none	0.06	1.05	Medicinical & Pharmaceutical Products	13.56	8.37
				Photographic Apparatus, Watches & Clocks	9.19	-0.53
Mexico	21 SITC 4-Digit product categories	0.23	0.17	Electrical Machinery & Apparatus	23.02	-0.82
				Road Vehicles	10.21	5.98

At the same time, export volumes of these countries to China are very low. While they have little to lose from China's accession in terms of third-market competition, they also have little to gain in terms of new markets. There was thus no need to speed up bilateral talks as for instance in the case of Chile, for which China constitutes a market of almost 5 % of their exports and which hence reached an agreement already in 1999.

For instance, from 1993 to 2002, the share of these industries' exports in total exports has dropped by an annual rate of 20 % respectively in Thailand. India's textiles industry, which on average accounts for 16.4 % of total national exports, has likewise decreased by 12.2 %. In light of such numbers it seems reasonable that these countries try to exclude a powerful exporting nation such as China from the world trade system and India has consequentially expressed major concerns for domestic industries – regardless if import- or export competing. More precisely, Indian officials tried to restrict Chinese membership rights in the WTO for "...more flexibility to take anti-dumping and safeguard measures against Chinese exports." (Financial Times, July 3, 2001).

While the temporizing of these countries can indeed be interpreted as a delay strategy for the protection of export-competing industries, this is comparably more difficult for the majority of the Latin American and Caribbean (LAC) countries which gave China the green light for accession in 2000, namely Argentina, Costa Rica, Ecuador and Guatemala (in the order of agreements reached). Except for Costa Rica, which possesses a relatively large and fast growing industry for computer parts, these countries' agricultural exports have little in common with China's fast growing manufacturing industries. At the same time, export volumes of these countries to China are very low. While they have little to lose from China's accession in terms of third-market competition, they also have little to gain in terms of new markets. There was thus no need to speed up bilateral talks as for instance in the case of Chile, for which China constitutes a market of almost 5 % of their exports and which hence reached an agreement already in 1999.

Ricart and Chang (2005) offer an alternative explanation for potential Latin American attitudes against China's integration despite relatively low levels of trade competition. With its economic opening in the course of WTO accession, the Chinese government attracted large scale foreign direct investments (FDI). Governments of some Latin American countries knew that they would not be capable of competing with China in granting foreign investors access to cheap labour and prosperous domestic markets. Hence, competing for FDI instead of competing for international market shares needs to be incorporated into the delay function of these countries and probably also for Mexico, which plays a special role China's WTO accession bargaining.

Mexico, the main exporting country of labour intense manufactures to the USA, exhibits a specialization in similar exporting goods as China and has delayed the accession process most among all other negotiation dyads. As expected for other countries, which converge with China economically and have shown to be rather reluctant in the accession process, the Mexican government adopted a protectionist attitude not only to insulate domestic import-competing sectors from the influx of cheap Chinese products, but also to secure preferential access for exporters to the US market vis-à-vis China (Financial Times, January 10, 2001; Financial Times, July 21, 2001; Financial Times, December 10, 2001).

Mexican delegates were the last ones seeking bilateral talks with China in 2001 – thus delaying accession by one year although all other WP members had paved the way for accession. Mexico was concerned about China's fast economic growth especially because third-market effects arise for a multitude of industries, and by no means only for labour intense textiles and clothing: 36 % of total Mexican exports originate in the three sectors electrical machinery (23 %), telecommunication apparatus (10 %) and automatic data processing machines (3 %). Relative exports of electrical machinery have thereby declined on average by 1 % between 1993 and 2002. While this sector accounts for 'only' 9 % of Chinese exports, it grew by almost 10 % annually. A similar pattern applies to the computer industry, which accounts for roughly 3 % of both economies' exports, but which grew annually by 17 % in China, but only by 5 % in Mexico relative to total exports.

These growth rates again indicate that newly industrialized countries, which also specialize in exports of more capital intense technical manufactures, are severely more affected by third-market competition than producers of labour intense textiles and clothing – especially when considering that textiles and clothing exports from China dropped by roughly 4 % respectively. Figure 5.3 reflects these developments. It depicts Chinese export shares in total exports and plots them versus their average annual growth rates relative to total exports between 1993 and 2002. I chose only significant exports, that is, those with a total share of more than two percent for the sake of lucidity.

Figure 5.3 China's Mean Export Power 1993-2002

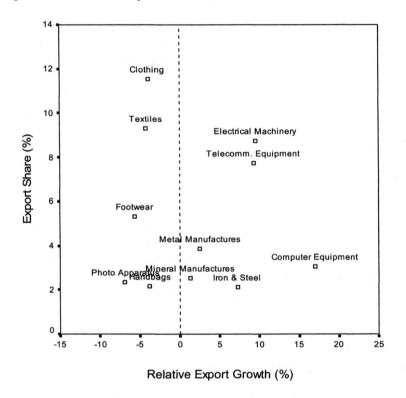

Figure 5.3 demonstrates that textiles and clothing account for the largest share of exports, but with negative growth rates. Instead, those industries which display double digit annual growth rates are more likely to challenge other exporters – including producers of electrical machinery from Thailand, Malaysia, Poland or Mexico. This again shows that it is not exclusively China's export power in textiles and clothing which challenges international producers of the same products, but the combined export power in clothing and the fast growing production of increasingly technical and capital intense goods.

Recent findings by Dani Rodrik (2006) confirm these results. Rodrik points out that China is not "… a simple story of specialization according to comparative advantage. While labour intensive exports (toys, garments, simple electronics assembly) have always played an important role in China's export basket, China also exports a wide range of highly sophisticated products. (…) China has somehow managed to latch on to advanced, high-productivity products that one would normally expect a poor, labor abundant country like China to produce, let alone exports." (Rodrik 2006: 4). Consequentially, it is rather the combination of export diversity and power, than simply the specialization in a few goods which increases third-market competition on a large scale, and which induces other governments to counteract further market opening by delaying China's WTO membership.

Mexico thereby not only demonstrates *that* governments are capable of delaying the accession process if the degree of competition is high, but this case also illuminates *how* delegates could drag on bilateral talks by one year by the extent of discriminatory measures they included in China's accession protocol.[30] Mexico managed to include a provision into the accession protocol, which practically offsets WTO anti-dumping rules for a multitude of goods within 21 different SITC 4-Digit industries for six years past China's accession (WTO 2001). This enables Mexican officials to continuously restrict imports by means of anti-dumping measures for many China-competing domestic industries. However, focusing on the bargaining strategy, this also reflects the disproportionately high demand for Chinese concessions, which also has been theorized to be the main mechanism for delaying negotiations. In the end, China partly made the concessions demanded by Mexico.

On the one hand, as these concessions consist of market access restrictions, Mexican import-competitors profit in the first place. On the other hand, delaying China's accession would not have been necessary for the sole purpose of protecting Mexican import-competitors. In the early 1990s, when China's WTO membership was still far ahead, already 11 % of Chinese exports to Mexico were restricted by antidumping measures (Niels and ten Kate 2004). Chapter 4

---

[30] Please note that detailed bilateral negotiation protocols are confidential. The only documents which are publicly accessible are the report of the working party and the final accession protocol. Unfortunately, none of these documents contains a closer description of the negotiation process for a potential identification of discriminatory demands against China. Instead, the accession protocol (WTO 2001) documents discriminatory outcomes in the form of restrictions of membership rights.

has shown that in the course of accession negotiations with China towards the late 1990s, Mexican AD practices against Chinese goods further increased. Together with the discriminatory measures stipulated in the accession protocol, Mexico now possesses enough legal tools to restrict imports from China on a large-scale. Thus, Mexican governments delayed China's accession due to the fear of increasing competition on third-markets.

5.3.2 Summing Up

This case study of the accession negotiations yields at delineating that (and how) third-market competition, which emerges out of countries' international economic integration, contributes to negotiation delay to the WTO. I do not question the standard explanations of delay in WTO accession negotiations, which mostly focus on the candidates' internal reform problems on the one hand and excessive demand for concessions by old members on the other. Instead, I have argued that governments have the incentive to strategically oppose China's WTO membership, since this is the only way of protecting exporters from increased competition with Chinese producers on third markets. Since the effect of third-market competition is only a small peace in the puzzle why China's accession has taken so long, it is difficult to isolate from other impact factors in the case study design. Nevertheless, with a careful interpretation of countries' export structures in comparison with their negotiation timing five key issues appear.

First, while the majority of its exports are still labor intense manufactures, China exhibits disproportionate large growth rates in more capital intense industries such as electrical machinery and computer parts. Accordingly, China will especially increase the international stress of competition within these industries and hence for countries which show a similar economic development. This applies to India, Thailand, Poland, Malaysia and Mexico – all of which belong to the group of last minute negotiators. Moreover, none of these delayers exports more than 4 % of its total exports to China. So while export-competition is strong, the fraction of exporters winning from China's membership is comparably small. South Korea, which already signed the bilateral agreement in 1997 also competes with China in primary export markets of electrical machinery *and* textiles, but its shares of exports directed to the People's Republic amounts to 11 %. For the Korean government it was hence, ceteris paribus, more important to gain quick access to Chinese markets than e.g. for India, with 2 % of total exports going to China.

Second, third-market competition does not mount into strategic delay if exclusively occurring on international textiles markets. China faces ongoing textiles import restrictions under the MFA, which regulates the phase out of the GATT agreement on textiles and clothing. These restrictions are subject to transition periods, but are also renegotiable: In 2005, the EU refreshed its quota system on textiles, which "…also provides a window for adaptation for producers in developing countries" (EU, 2005b). MFA regulations hence protect WTO textiles exporter vis-à-vis China past its accession. This logic is closely connected to the finding that primary importers of textiles and clothing, such as EU member states, grant preferential access to their principal suppliers, that is, to their Eastern European and Mediterranean neighbors. This explains for instance why Turkey paved China's way to the WTO early in the negotiations process despite the overall high level of export similarity.

Third, a number of special cases appear in the group of late negotiators in a sense that they have only little in common with China in terms of their export structures. This applies especially to Argentina, Ecuador and Guatemala, which neither show overall export similarities, nor specialization in China-competing sectors. Instead, agricultural products account for large fractions of their exports. Searching for alternative explanations, I highlighted the international competition in foreign direct investments, which have increasingly been redirected towards China in the late 1990s. As the Chinese government improved the domestic climate for investments, other newly industrialized and developing economies feared the withdrawal of foreign capital (Ricart and Chang 2005). Knowing that WTO accession further improves conditions for FDI inflows, this must also be considered as an incentive to bloc Chinese membership.

Fourth, the so called quad countries play a crucial role for the timing of China's accession. Especially the governments of the USA and EU member states have taken a leading role in the negotiations. Their signing of bilateral agreements can be considered as a green-light signal for other WTO members to sign contracts as well. They have not only negotiated Chinese concessions in the field of trade in goods, but also demanded large-scale commitments for the protection of intellectual property rights and the opening of service sectors. It is all the more surprising that a number of countries furthered delayed China's accession after all critical issues had been settled among China and the quad countries.

This leads directly to the fifth outstanding issue of China's accession process. Among all negotiation partners, the Mexican government was most reluctant to integrate China into the world trade system. The Mexican demand for Chinese concessions was so far-fetched, which China did not agree upon until they finally worked out a compromise by the end of 2001. One of the reasons is most certainly that Mexico's export structure is very similar to that of China, from clothing to computer parts. The same applies to their primary target market: The USA. So while Mexico manages to protect it import-competitors from an influx of Chinese goods with a flood of antidumping and safeguard regulations, this is not possible for exporters competing with Chinese goods within the USA.

Keeping China out of the WTO would have been beneficiary for Mexico, but in the end the outside pressure for its acceptance grew too strong. The Mexican government nevertheless solely managed to drag off China's accession by more than one year, when all critical issues had for long been solved between China and all other working party members. The logic of third-market competition as an incentive for strategic accession delay is hence best observable in the case of Mexico versus China.

5.4 Concluding Remarks

China's path to the WTO took 15 years and was cumbersome. Previous research enumerates a number of stumbling blocs in the accession process. Reforming China from a centrally planned to a market oriented economy within a communist political system is for instance challenging but necessary to align China's trade policies with WTO rules. Reform took its time, and so did the accession process. This was complemented by Chinese political incidents such as the Beijing Massacre at Tiananmen Square in 1989. As a result, the Chinese government fell from grace with the international community and was also punished with a postponement of its integration into the world trade system.

This Chapter does not doubt that these factors have had significant impact on China's long way to the WTO. I nevertheless argue that one factor has largely been neglected: increasing third-market competition. The integration of China's powerful economy increases competition for import-competing industries domestically and for export-oriented-industries on third-markets. While Chapter 4 demonstrated governments' capability of limiting import-competition with contingent protection, the theoretical part of this Chapter showed that traditional trade policies cannot limit third-market competition because it emerges abroad as a consequence of other members' trade agreements with the Chinese government. Hence, the magnitude of increasing competition is not directly negotiable for governments of affected countries. Excluding the China from the WTO by strategically delaying accession negotiations is therefore an effective tool to prolong quota rents for exporters vis-à-vis non-member competitors. However, delay is finite: the candidate can join the organization under the acceptance of discriminatory membership rights, which diminish negative effects from increased competition for other members.

Third-market competition has in fact triggered crucial conflicts in the case of the accession of The People's Republic of China to the WTO in 2001 – as empirically demonstrated in the explorative case study. Delineating the 15 year long accession process revealed that China itself largely delayed its accession with the slow pace of economic reform and with its loss of international credibility followed by the Beijing Massacre at Tiananmen Square in 1989. Protective attitudes of import-competing interests in the USA and the European Union further protracted the accession process. In addition to these traditional explanations, the case study revealed the theoretically predicted demand for discriminatory measures by countries with homogenous export structures relative to China. Especially Mexico has shown to be a reluctant negotiator in bilateral market access talks, with high demands for trade distorting measures on Chinese products in the case of its delayed accession. Mexican exporters feared to lose their preferential access to the US under the North American Free Trade Agreement.

In most general terms, countries were reluctant to accept China as a new member WTO member if they face high degrees of export competition in more advanced technical products, which exhibit large growth rates in China, if they simultaneously are not naturally protected by preferential access to their target markets or by MFA trade restrictions on Chinese textiles and if they additionally deliver only small percentages of their exports to China. Besides the crucial Mexican case, these countries are India, Malaysia, Thailand, and Poland. However, Argentina, Ecuador and Guatemala are also last minute negotiators and contradict the logic of export competition as their focus on agricultural products has nothing in common with China's export structure. As a plausible alternative explanations of these results I have pointed to the findings of Ricart and Chang (2005), who find out that Latin American countries compete with China for FDI.

From a methodological perspective the case study demonstrated the difficulties of isolating the theorized effect. Holding ceteris paribus conditions constant is a heroic undertaking which renders causal inference almost impossible. This is aggravated by the difficulty of obtaining reliable information on individual bilateral negotiations. Official protocols are highly classified by the WTO, which only leaves the information given at press conferences and gathered in press reports. This case study is nevertheless the first assessment of systematically sketching the timing of bilateral accession negotiations under the assumption that China's long way to the WTO is *intended* by other members due to the international competition it causes. Moreover, the argument that export-competition instead of import-competition triggers major negotiation conflicts explains the immense participation of *equally endowed* newly industrialized economies in China's accession process.

Emerging third-market competition thus adds an additional source of conflict to WTO accession negotiations, not only in the case of China. However, the accession of the People's Republic of China to the WTO is a crucial case. The growing export power and diversity is unique compared to other economies which have joined the WTO since 1995. Accordingly, the magnitude of third-market competition arising from its accession is larger than in other accession cases. Nevertheless, the simple fact that the mechanisms are pronounced in China's case does not automatically render them invalid for smaller states. The case of China can be generalized to WTO accession processes in that the degree of third-market competition is a function of export power and diversity. Consequentially, negotiation conflicts are absent for economically insignificant states, which also applies to conflicts arising from increased import-competition.

Considering economically more powerful accession countries, such as Russia or Ukraine, the impact of increasing competition for exporters on the bargaining strategies of similarly endowed countries has far reaching consequences for the length and complexity of WTO accession: remaining non-members face not only membership opposition from high-income nations, but also from similar countries attacking them from behind to prevent income losses for their export-oriented corporations. Acceding to the WTO will therefore become an increasingly lengthy matter.

In sum, the previous Chapters reveal the magnitude of opposition China faced during its accession process, regardless whether in the form of antidumping and contingent protection or in the form of negotiation delay. Eventually, compromises on both sides led to China's membership in 2001. Since then, the People's Republic itself is entitled to participate in WTO dispute settlement proceedings and file antidumping measures against other members as well as outsiders. The puzzling question of the next Chapter is if this now mounts into China retaliating against those countries which have previously aggravated the accession process. More specifically, I first explore if China follows a tit-for-tat strategy with respect to antidumping measures. Second, I examine if China's membership has indeed caused a flood of trade disputes as has been predicted in previous research, and if yes, if these disputes are again retaliatory in nature.

6 PAST ACCESSION: CHINA'S CURRENT STATUS IN THE WTO

This book so far focussed on the conflicts emerging in China's WTO accession negotiations. I have shown that international opposition against China's economic integration coupled with domestic problems of bringing the Chinese economy in line with WTO rules accounted for limited membership rights and a delay of the accession process. Today, a fairly long time has passed since accession in 2001. Over the past years, China has reduced domestic trade barriers and profits in return for improved foreign market access. Membership now also entitles Chinese officials to bring unfair foreign trade practices on the agenda of the dispute settlement body and entitles individual industries to defend themselves with antidumping and safeguard complaints. Hence, today the tools that were utilized to limit Chinese trade flows during the accession process are now also accessible to China.

This chapter evaluates China's utilization of its newly won membership rights. Considering the opposition it faced during the accession process, special attention is paid to a retaliatory pattern of China's membership practices: do Chinese officials now utilize its membership to retaliate against those members, who have previously aggravated accession negotiations? This chapter hence sketches China's response to the membership opposition identified in earlier chapters.

More specifically, Chapter 4 demonstrated that overt demand for discrimination was magnified by contingent protection in the form of antidumping regulations, which enabled governments to promote liberalization with China and its accession without upsetting import-competitors. While the antidumping strategy partly solved redistributive conflicts with regard to import-competitors, Chapter 5 has highlighted a third emerging conflict in China's accession negotiations when exporters also suffer from increased international competition. I have theoretically outlined and empirically demonstrated that governments with large fractions of their exporters being affected by Chinese competition delay the accession process. No other efficient solution to protect exporting industries on foreign markets exists.

The accession process took 15 years not only due to home-made reform reluctance and consequential incompatibility with WTO rules, but also due to major opposition from established developing and developed WTO members. Since 2001, China has had equal rights within the international trade community with full access to the WTO dispute settlement body and the right to file anti-dumping measures against 'unfair' foreign dumping practices. Is the Chinese government finally fighting back by the same means? I argue that since China is a member of the WTO, its government is pressured by domestic industries not to open domestic markets too far. The Chinese government now has the same tools of contingent protection at hand as any other WTO member country. At the same time, Chinese officials now have access to the WTO dispute settlement body in cases where they suspect other countries of unfair trade practices. In sum, this chapter answers the question to which degree China makes use of its newly won membership rights and if China today displays a retaliatory behaviour through antidumping measures and trade disputes against those WTO members, which have previously responded with protectionism during its membership ambitions.

To answer these questions, I first draw on previous research that has empirically confirmed a tit-for-tat strategy of international antidumping users. Empirical findings show that WTO members who make excessive use of antidumping filings exclusively target these measures at other WTO antidumping users. Moreover, within this antidumping club, members tend to especially restrict imports in a retaliatory manner, that is, they file antidumping measures against countries which have targeted them in the past (Prusa, 2001; Prusa and Skeath, 2001, 2004). Considering the massive antidumping measures China faced during its accession, I argue that, as a new WTO member, China will act accordingly, that is, use antidumping duties as retaliation against those members who have previously restricted imports from China.

Second, I focus on China's future role in the WTO dispute settlement system. Prior to China's WTO accession, much speculation occurred with respect to its impact on international trade disputes. Scholars argued that China's economic power and the partly incomplete transformation from a centrally planned to market based economy will trigger a flood of complaints to the dispute settlement body against China (Ostry 2003; Jackson 2003). I additionally argue that, analogous to increasing antidumping retaliation, Chinese officials are also inclined to increasingly utilize the dispute settlement body to complain against those members who opposed its WTO membership in the first place.

The empirical descriptions reveal that China has indeed become an active user of antidumping measures. However, China does not retaliate against other WTO members, but follows the club-rule of WTO antidumping practices (Finger 1993), that is, it only targets other antidumping users. After having demonstrated China's activities in the WTO anti-dumping club, I round off the description of China's past WTO accession stance by illustrating its participation in the dispute settlement system, which is not retaliatory at all: China has only twice been directly involved into WTO disputes – as complainant and defendant respectively.

However, a closer look at the cases uncovers that the Chinese dispute participation as a third-party skyrocketed immediately after its accession in 2001, thereby allowing China to take advantage of its newly won membership rights. The results also show that other countries abstained from complaining against China. This contradicts predictions in previous research, assuming a flood of trade complaints against China past its accession (Ostry 2003; Jackson 2003), and it also contradicts my expectations of China defending itself through trade disputes.

The remainder of this chapter is organized as follows. The subsequent part sketches retaliation strategies between WTO anti-dumping users and argues, that also China must be expected to increase its antidumping activities, thereby joining the WTO antidumping club. Thereafter, the empirical description of China's anti-dumping pattern as a new WTO member reveals that it has become an active member of the anti-dumping community, but contradicts the expectations of a retaliatory behaviour. The same pattern will be identified in the last section dealing with China's dispute activity: China participates in WTO disputes as a third-party without provoking other members with direct complaints.

6.1 China and the WTO Antidumping Club

The filing of antidumping duties on imports from other countries has – in Chapter 3 – already been identified as a modern form of protectionism, which gained prominence since not infringing WTO rules. In sum "...the empirical studies which analyse the operation of the anti-dumping system find that the AD system is basically a flexible tool for preventing imports, whether dumped or not, from causing injury to domestic industry." (Messerlin and Tharakan 1999: 1258).

Only a small fraction of all WTO members are antidumping users and surprisingly, these countries primarily file AD measures on goods from other AD users.

According to Finger (1993), those countries utilize the WTO AD regulation to restrict imports form a relatively stable club in which they only impose measures on one another. During the 1980s, "Two-thirds of anti-dumping investigations are within the club – against exports from a country that is also an antidumper" (Finger 1993: 7). The nature of this antidumping club changed in the 1990s with more and more developing and industrializing countries using AD measures, but the results remain valid: Even 'new' and developing AD users tend to direct their measures towards other club members (Prusa and Skeath 2001; 2004).

Moreover, within this antidumping club, members have been found to develop a retaliatory behaviour, by which they file AD measures against exactly those countries, which have targeted them in the past (Prusa, 2001; Prusa and Skeath, 2001, 2004). Arguing that this practice is based on punishing other WTO members for this form of trade distortion, Prusa and Skeath (2004: 15) differentiate between 'tit-for-tat punishment' and 'club effect punishment'.

In more general terms, the first strategy refers to direct retaliatory behaviour in which country A's application of AD measures against country B causes B to use AD against A. The second 'club effect' punishment describes a situation in which the AD measures filed by A against B trigger other countries to also use AD against B.

Unfortunately, the authors lack closer explanations for the motives behind this empirically observed behaviour. Thus, why should the Chinese government act accordingly, that is, apply a tit-for-tat strategy in the WTO antidumping club? To answer this question, I first clarify the incentives of using AD in general. Thereafter, I argue that once the decision to allow the limitation of imports through AD duties has been taken, it is easier to direct them at other experienced AD users instead of provoking a tit-for-tat reaction of yet another WTO member.

During its accession, China has become the main target of antidumping measures without having the opportunity to retaliate as a WTO outsider. Its membership now enables China to also take advantage of antidumping regulation as a legal form of protecting import-competing markets. Its newly won WTO membership simultaneously requires ongoing trade liberalization and the opening of domestic market. Today, China can utilize antidumping measures to protect special domestic industries while liberalizing trade for others. More specifically, China's membership conditions, which were negotiated in numerous bilateral and multilateral agreements, require the Chinese government to substantially open markets for liberalized trade. As any other trade-liberalizing country, this must be enforced against the will of losing, mostly import-competing industries.

China's tendency to use AD measures thus follows the logic of 'contingent protection' elaborated on in Chapter 4: By using AD measures, the Chinese government satisfies special protectionist demands while liberalizing trade for free-trade oriented industries. This minimizes domestic opposition to liberal trade policies, equivalent to the rise of AD measures in other developing countries, where "...anti-dumping constitutes a necessary 'safety valve' that allows policy makers in these countries to maintain political support for broader trade liberalization initiatives" (Niels and ten Kate, 2004: 969).

From this perspective, China starts its AD activity for the same reasons as countries which responded protectionist to its accession: they practiced contingent protection to minimize domestic opposition against liberalized trade with China as I have shown in Chapter 4. International demand for economic opening hence positively affects domestic contingent protection. In the case of China, the need for accelerated tariff cuts past its WTO accession is therefore also accompanied by an increase in antidumping measures. The pure existence of antidumping incentives does however not per se explain incentives to retaliate. Thus, why should the Chinese government be inclined to direct AD activities at other AD users, as predicted by the club-effect hypothesis, or with a tit-for-tat strategy at exactly those countries which have previously restricted Chinese exports with contingent protection?

Assume that the extensive use of import restrictions harms economic relations between China and its trading partners. Consider that a given country, e.g. India, starts damaging trade relations to China during its accession process by largely levying AD duties on imports. The day of accession now enables China to likewise file AD duties. The Chinese government, pressured to protect domestic import-competitors and knowing that India shares the common understanding that AD measures are a legitimate tool of protection, hence reciprocally levies AD duties on goods from India. In other words: If trade relations with extensive AD users are already damaged, why challenging friendly trade partners?

Given a traditional AD user is a major exporter of the product to be protected, Chinese authorities will not levy duties on the like products of a non-AD user. This is magnified by the fact that AD measures against countries that have previously harmed China's exports are easier to justify – at home and abroad. Domestic and international free-traders less likely condemn contingent protection if it happens on a reciprocal basis (tit-for-tat) or at least if these measures harm other protectionist countries (club effect).

Following this logic, China is expected to also join the antidumping club by filing AD duties relatively more on goods from those countries, which have previously targeted Chinese products during the accession process.

The subsequent empirical observations on China's antidumping practices since 2002 reveal that among all WTO members, AD measures have in fact exclusively filed against other antidumpers. A retaliatory behaviour can however not be confirmed and China also levies AD duties on goods originating in non-WTO countries, that is, the club hypothesis only holds for the sub-sample of WTO member states.

6.2 China's Antidumping Practices: Empirical Observations

As outlined in the previous section, Prusa and Skeath (2004) hypothesized and confirmed a tit-for-tat strategy of antidumping filings among WTO members. I argue, that given its troublesome entry to the WTO, the Chinese government must also be inclined to join the antidumping club (Finger 1993) and to file AD measures at those countries, which have targeted China before. Thus, do the findings by Prusa and Skeath (2004) also apply to China since 2002? Does China participate in the WTO anti-dumping club, in which members exclusively file AD measures towards one another and does China tend to retaliate against previous AD attacks by those members? In a descriptive manner, Table 6.1 sheds light on these questions. It contains general information about all countries which have filed AD measures between January 1995 and June 2005 (AD-users) and about those which have been targeted by Chinese measures between January 2002 and June 2005 without having applied measures themselves (non-AD-users).

Table 6.1   China's AD Practices Past Accession

AD-Users	AD by initiating Country				AD by China	
	Total 1995-2005	Total targeted at China	Targeted at China 1995-2001	Share in total AD (%)	Total 2002-2005	Share (%)
India	309	63	39	12.6	2	3.2
United States	229	50	31	13.5	9	14.5
European Union	200	33	26	13.0	10	16.1
Argentina	139	33	23	16.5	0	0
South Africa	113	14	12	10.6	0	0
Brazil	63	12	10	15.9	0	0
Venezuela	25	11	10	40.0	0	0
Turkey	81	29	9	11.1	0	0
Peru	38	13	8	21.1	0	0
Canada	84	11	6	7.1	0	0
Republic of Korea	44	10	6	13.6	14	22.6
Mexico	71	11	4	5.6	1	1.6
Australia	65	6	4	6.2	0	0
Colombia	13	3	2	15.4	0	0
Philippines	9	2	2	22.2	0	0
Poland	9	2	2	22.2	0	0
Egypt	30	3	1	3.3	0	0
Indonesia	23	2	1	4.3	1	1.6
Trinidad and Tobago	7	2	1	14.3	0	0
Chile	6	1	1	16.7	0	0
Israel	15	1	1	6.7	0	0
Malaysia	21	1	1	4.8	2	3.2
Thailand	25	2	0	0.0	0	0
Jamaica	4	1	0	0.0	0	0
New Zealand	17	1	0	0.0	0	0
Chinese Taipei	2	0	0	0.0	4	6.5
Costa Rica	1	0	0	0.0	0	0
Czech Republic	1	0	0	0.0	0	0
Guatemala	1	0	0	0.0	0	0
Japan	3	0	0	0.0	11	17.7
Latvia	1	0	0	0.0	0	0
Lithuania	7	0	0	0.0	0	0
Nicaragua	1	0	0	0.0	0	0
Pakistan	6	0	0	0.0	0	0
Paraguay	1	0	0	0.0	0	0
Singapore	2	0	0	0.0	1	1.6
Uruguay	1	0	0	0.0	0	0
China	62					
Total	1729	317	200	11.6	55	88.7
Non-AD-Users						
Russia	0	0		0	4	6.5
Iran	0	0		0	1	1.6
Kazakhstan	0	0		0	1	1.6
Ukraine	0	0		0	1	1.6
Total	0	0		0	7	11.3

Source: WTO antidumping database[31]

---

[31] Accessible at http://www.wto.org/english/tratop_e/adp_e/adp_e.htm.

The second column displays these countries' total number of ADs, the third column the total number of measures targeted at China from 1995 to 2005, followed by measures which have been filed against Chinese goods prior its accession in 2001 and their shares in total measures. China's AD pattern past its accession until June 2005 is captured in the last two columns, with first the total number of AD measures applied against the respective country and their percentage share in total Chinese measures within this timeframe.

The countries which have applied large numbers of AD measures against China between 1995 and 2001 vary remarkably with respect to income and region. India has for instance levied antidumping duties on goods originating in China in 39 cases, the United States in 31 and the EU in 26 cases. In relative numbers, Venezuela yields the highest score with 40 % of total AD activity being directed at Chinese goods. In total, a heterogeneous set of 22 countries filed antidumping complaints against China between 1995 and 2001. Another 15 countries of the antidumping club abstained from ADs against China prior 2001, but have been active AD users against at least one other country.

China itself quickly joined the AD club past its accession: In 2002, AD measures were levied on imports in 5 cases. Figures skyrocketed to 33 cases in 2003 before dropping back to 14 cases in 2004 and 10 cases in the first half of 2005. The last two columns of Table 6.1 reveal that out of these 62 AD cases, 88.7 % have been directed at other AD users. Almost half of total Chinese AD actions (48.3 %) have thereby been applied to the EU, USA and Japan.

The remaining activities were distributed among relatively new AD users, with 22.6 % of all Chinese activities directed against goods from South Korea and further minor fractions at Chinese Taipei, India, Malaysia, Mexico, Indonesia and Singapore. Only 11 % of AD activities were applied on goods from four non-AD-users, namely Russia, Iran, Kazakhstan and Ukraine, who are also non-WTO members.

Hence, among all WTO members, China uses AD measures exclusively against other AD users, plus a minor share against non-AD-users, which are also WTO outsiders. This clearly supports the argument of the club-effect of AD usage, but do these figures also reflect a retaliatory pattern?

Although China targeted cumulative 34 % of its AD activities at its top three antidumpers, India, the USA and the EU, clear evidence of a retaliatory strategy does not appear: At the other end of the scale, China also applied 26 % of AD duties against countries which previously *abstained* from attacking China. China's antidumping practices are therefore far from being reciprocal. A strong reaction to the extensive historical AD use by other countries appears only in three cases: The USA, the EU and South Korea. Past its accession, China filed 9 AD duties against the USA as a potential reaction to 31 measures initiated by US authorities between 1995 and 2001. This relationship is similar to that of the EU: China responds with 10 measures to 26 initiated by the European Union. The AD user targeted most by China is South Korea: 22.6 % of China's AD activity aims at restricting imports from Korea, which prior applied only 6 measures on Chinese goods.

Among the group of AD users, China has in sum utilized contingent protection against 7 countries, which prior acted accordingly. However this result stands in sharp contrast to no Chinese AD activity against 11 countries, which have applied more than 10 % of their AD duties against China between 1995 and 2001. Plus, China restricted imports from close trading partners, i.e. Chinese Taipei, Japan and Singapore, which have not targeted China at all during its accession process. The information given hence by no means reveals a general Chinese tit-for-tat strategy. Instead, with exception of the EU, the USA, Mexico and the WTO outsiders, China's entire AD activity is directed at regional trading partners.

China's AD activity past accession appears to be *independent* from the previous AD behaviour of its trading partners. The hypothesized tit-for-tat strategy observed in the cases of other WTO members must hence be rejected in the Chinese case. Nevertheless, China strictly follows the rules of the AD club with not a single AD duty filed on goods from non-AD-users, except for the non-users, non-WTO members. Especially with respect to the applicants Ukraine and Russia, China itself now practices protectionist responses to future WTO members.

Besides post accession AD activity, China also gained the right to bring unfair foreign trade policies before the WTO dispute settlement body. The next section illustrates China's participation in international trade disputes. Special attention is paid to predictions in previous research that China's accession to the WTO significantly influences the number of trade disputes and to the question if China increasingly files complaints against its membership opponents.

6.3 China's Accession and WTO Trade Disputes

One of the benefits cited most for developing and newly industrialized countries to accede to the WTO is the improved access to the dispute settlement body (e.g. Michalopoulos 1998; Yang 1999). This is also one of the primary motives of China to join the WTO, as the Chinese chief negotiator Long Yongtu (2000: 39) points out:

"When conflicts or contradictions arise, the WTO has a mechanism by which conflicts may be resolved. This is known as the arbitration committee, which serves to judge and determine who is right and who is wrong when two member nations are in conflict. I feel that once we have joined the WTO, it would be to our advantage to have available to us such a mechanism for the resolution of multilateral conflicts of interest. For instance, if there is to be a fight between a big, bulky fellow and a skinny, little guy, would it be to the small fellow's advantage for the fight to take place in some dark corner, or would it be better for him to have the fight take place out in the open, in the public eye?"

Besides the curiosity of Long Yongtu perceiving China, one of the world's largest trading nations, as a "little guy" (Long Yongtu 2000: 39), this citation indicates China's ambitions to use the WTO dispute settlement mechanism for solving international trade disputes for two reasons. First, it enables China to defend itself against complaints by other countries, which are likely to increase due to China's incomplete transition from a centrally planned to a market based economy.

Second, the ongoing demand for trade restrictions against Chinese goods gives rise to suspicion that protectionist governments continue to search for loopholes in WTO AD regulations to further apply tariff and non-tariff barriers on Chinese imports. In this respect, the dispute settlement body (DSB) gives China itself the opportunity to complain against such measures. Chinese officials could for instance litigate on the basis of unjustified antidumping and safeguard practices, or file complaints against those members, who obstructed its accession process.

In sum, its accession to the WTO in 2001 now enables Chinese trade policy makers to bring trade distorting measures, which are neither legitimized in the accession protocol, nor justified under any other exception to the rule of non-discrimination, before the dispute settlement body. Thus, the number of trade disputes theoretically increases past China's accession for two reasons. First, equivalent to earlier considerations, China can utilize the DSB for retaliation against those countries, which have complicated its way to the WTO. Following this logic, the Chinese government would primarily complain against ostensible 'unfair' trade practices of the top antidumpers or against those, who have delayed the accession process.

Second, there is also a high probability that China will, in the long run, find itself in the role of the defendant in a "flood of disputes" (Ostry 2003: 37). This argument is rooted in the remaining unsettled issues of Chinese reform. Especially the persistence of state owned enterprises, ongoing subsidization and critical issues such as service sector liberalization and the protection of intellectual property rights open the floodgates for foreign trade complaints against China.

A contrary view of China's impact on the DSB is that other members will be cautious in complaining against China because, yet again, of the fear of Chinese retaliation. According to this view, industries and governments would prefer informal talks instead of provoking trade conflicts with powerful China (Ostry 2003). In the short run past accession, the number of trade disputes involving China is also limited by the transitional status of Chinese membership, which makes it "...very hard to establish a violation case, so the transition clauses will are going to be crucial in preventing too much of a rush to litigation." (Jackson 2003).

In the long run however, Jackson (2003) expects an increase in disputes *against* China simply because "China is a large economy, and large economies face large numbers of cases" (Jackson 2003: 27). After a short introduction into the dispute procedure, the remaining part will clarify the question whether China indeed plays a crucial role in the DSB past its accession in 2001, either as complainant or as defendant.

6.4 China's Trade Dispute Participation: Empirical Observations

WTO members can basically participate in trade disputes in three different ways: As a complainant, defendant or third-party. Trade disputes start with the request for consultations, in which the complainant files its objections with respect to specific trade policies conducted by the defendant. What follows is a 60 day long consultation period enabling the parties involved to informally solve the conflict before litigation. 46 % of all WTO disputes are already solved during this consultation phase (Busch and Reinhardt 2006: 7).

In the remaining cases, the complainant usually starts the formal litigation by requesting the formation of a panel. If the conflict is still not resolved during this proceeding, the panel renders a judgment, which then needs to be adopted by the WTO. If the defendant finally does not manage to bring its disputed trade policy in accordance with WTO rules, the complainant is authorized to retaliate against the defendant (Busch and Reinhardt 2006).

Countries that also feel affected by the trade policies under dispute are free to join the settlement process as third-parties. Third-party countries issue their views on the subject in the various settlement stages and can thereby indirectly impact the outcome of the dispute. They are generally allowed to participate in the panel if they claim to have a 'substantial interest' in the dispute, and are also welcome to the consultation phase if they assure having a 'substantial trade interest' (WTO n.d.).

Third parties thus informally influence the dispute in the early consultation phase, or express their views during the panel proceeding. Third-parties are mostly countries with a "substantial economic stake in the litigation" (Bown 2005: 291), and have been found to significantly impact dispute outcomes.[32] Participating in trade disputes as third-party is therefore an efficient way of impacting dispute outcomes: It requires less administrative workload and is consequentially less costly than initiating trade disputes in the role of the complainant. Participating as third-party also reduces the risk of trade conflicts and retaliation by the defendant. Third-party countries thus free-ride on the ambitions of the initiating country.

Contrary to the expectations of China triggering a case-flood of trade disputes in the WTO, as of February 2006 it has only been directly involved into two trade disputes. In 2002, Chinese officials complained against US safeguard measures on imports of certain steel products. The Chinese government thus took immediate advantage of its WTO membership by trying to improve its access to the US steel market, supported by 14 further third-countries. As a result, the USA terminated all safeguards under dispute in December 2003 (WTO DS252).

In 2004, and potentially as a reaction to this first Chinese complaint, the USA filed a complaint against China, objecting that Chinese manufactures of 'inte-

---

[32] Busch and Reinhardt (2006) determine that the participation of third parties in the consultation phase inhibits an early solution of the dispute. Instead, disputes with third party involvement are more likely to be transferred to a panel proceeding than disputes without third parties.

grated circuits' were entitled to partial refunds of the value added tax on their products. This dispute was however settled within the 60 days of the consultation period: China quickly agreed to eliminate the objected preferential taxes (WTO DS309).

Given China's fast growing export industries and its involvement in international trade, its seemingly weak involvement in trade disputes comes as a surprise. Considering the small timeframe of only four years since its accession, it is likely that members still grant China a period of grace. Due to its economic power, a long term absence from trade disputes seems however unrealistic, especially when considering that Chinese officials have all the more been active as third-party in WTO dispute consultations and panels.

So while China is still cautious in filing direct trade complaints to the WTO, it is – since 2002 – one of the most active third-party participants in informal dispute consultations as well as in panels. For exemplification, Figure 6.1 displays the total number of annually initiated trade disputes by WTO members relative to the number of those cases in which China participated as third-party, which skyrocketed in 2002, directly after its accession to the WTO.

Figure 6.1   China's Participation in Trade Disputes 1995-2005

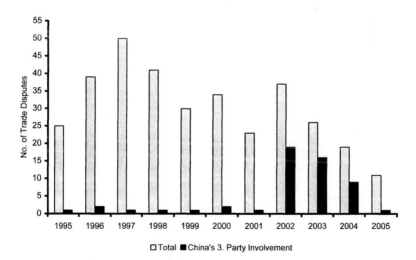

□ Total ■ China's 3. Party Involvement

Over the years past accession, China's relative third-party participation remained stable, despite the decreasing number of total trade disputes. Until 2004, Chinese officials acted as the third-party in the majority of the dispute cases. China has hence rapidly taken advantage of the improved access to the dispute settlement body while simultaneously shying away from directly initiating litigation – at least until today.

Given the finding that third-parties can indeed impact dispute outcomes especially when they act early in the consultation phase (Busch and Reinhardt 2006), this is an optimal strategy for China as a new member to the WTO. Third-party participation enables officials to affect dispute verdicts to their advantage on the one hand, without provoking retaliation on the other. It is thus less risky than filing complaints directly to the WTO. China's strategy in the dispute cases is therefore similar to its antidumping activities: Taking advantage of the newly won rights without directly attacking or retaliating against other members.

The following example additionally illustrates the Chinese free-rider incentives for third-party involvement. In 2002, Brazil objected US subsidies to domestic cotton producers – a trade distorting measure which also adversely affected Chinese textile exports to the USA. China and a number of other, mostly developing countries, received third-party rights for their participation in the dispute to achieve a verdict against US subsidies. Although the panel report has not been finalized yet and the dispute continues, the USA came under significant pressure to reduce cotton subsidies.

In 2005, "the United States stated its intention to comply with the recommendations and rulings of the DSB in a manner that respected its WTO obligations and had already begun evaluating options for doing so, and stated that it would require a reasonable period of time to implement the recommendation and ruling of the DSB." (WTO DS267). Eventually, third-party countries of this dispute and Brazil, the initiator, will profit likewise from the elimination of subsidies. The difference is however that Brazil now faces an increased probability of being retargeted by future US complaints and that Brazil bears the lion's share of litigation costs.

Although an increase of complaints by and against China was expected, it seems that both sides – China *and* old members – are fearful of retaliatory disputes and that its recent membership still accounts for the postponement of complaints against China. Since membership rights are already limited during this transition period, Chinese officials try to avert trade conflicts which would potentially lead to further trade restrictions. Thus, third-party acting past its accession is the best way to impact trade conflicts and to free-ride on the verdicts fought out between other countries, without bearing the risk of future retaliation and consequentially further trade restrictions.

This modest form of utilizing its newly won WTO membership rights is similar to the pattern revealed for China's antidumping practices. China acts in a club-like manner by filing AD duties exclusively against other WTO antidumpers, but it does not initiate AD measures for the motive of punishing other members for previous duties on Chinese goods. China confirms the empirically finding of an AD club, with WTO members only utilizing AD measures against other antidumpers, but contradicts earlier findings showing a tendency towards retaliatory behaviour, that is, applying a tit-for-tat strategy of antidumping (Prusa and Skeath 2004).

In sum, these observations lead to the conclusion that China is – with respect to antidumping practices and dispute involvement – a cooperative and cautious new WTO member. The case-flood of trade disputes oftentimes associated with China's accession does not yet appear. The total number of trade disputes and the number of antidumping measures initiated by China also decrease drastically since 2002. If this remains the case in the long run is difficult to predict.

It seems however likely that China's accelerated economic growth, the shift from the production of labour intensive to more capital intensive manufactures and the accompanied increasing competition for industrial countries will trigger more trade disputes once the Chinese economy is fully integrated. The evolution of China's role in the WTO hence remains tantalizing and deserves future observation and analysis beyond this book's scope.

7 CONCLUSION

China's accession to the WTO – as many others – has been lengthy and burdensome. It seems intuitively puzzling that one of the largest and the fastest growing trading nations was excluded from the world trading system despite its 15 year long ambitions to join. Previous research dealing with this puzzle – regardless whether for transition economies in general or China in particular – explain stumbling blocs in the WTO accession process as a consequence of applicants' reform reluctance, incompatibility of centrally planned economies with market based WTO rules, excessive demand for applicants' tariff concessions to maximize foreign market access, political incidences or the nature of the WTO accession procedure. Each of these institutional factors impacts the length and outcome of WTO accessions, but they cannot fully account for the conflicts inherent to China's membership negotiations.

This analysis seeks to complement the WTO accession literature by taking a different stance on the matter. I analysed why and how redistributive effects emerging from multilateral trade liberalization at the heart of the WTO's accession process cause protectionist responses to and the delay of the integration of economically powerful countries into the world trade system. I argue that governments try to protect powerful export- and import-competing industries. Governments dominated by influential import-competitors demand ongoing trade restrictions against the applicant country and utilize legal WTO antidumping regulations to replace common import-tariffs by industry-specific protection. In other words, protectionist governments successively substitute historical import-tariffs on goods originating in the candidate's economy by antidumping measures with an increasing probability of the candidate's accession. While this ongoing 'contingent protection' minimizes the opposition of import-competitors, governments face significant difficulties in protecting exporters from increased competition on world markets. This situation, dubbed third-market competition, causes governments to delay bilateral accession negotiations and the date of enlargement to prolong quota rents vis-à-vis the candidate's exporters abroad.

A close examination of the 15 year-long WTO accession negotiations, which were completed in 2001, of The Peoples Republic of China served to illustrate and test the theoretical considerations. Panel regressions analysed the determinants and the trends of protectionist responses to China's WTO application in the form of industry-specific antidumping measures throughout the 1990s. A case study of China's WTO accession further illustrates the impact of third-market competition on individual bilateral liberalization negotiations. The results confirm first, that the redistributive effects for import-competitors foster increasing protectionism by means of antidumping measures. The focussed protection of powerful industries reduces the opposition against enlargement and enables the accession of new members to the WTO with limited membership benefits. If, second, the applicant's exporters cause increasing competition on third-markets for a multitude of domestic exporting corporations, governments of affected economies delay bilateral negotiations and the enlargement.

This concluding chapter summarizes the theoretical arguments and connects them to the empirical findings. The results are analysed with respect to their generalizability beyond China's accession and their potential to identify conflicts in current accession negotiations with Russia and Vietnam.

7.1 General Results in a Broader Perspective

Under the baseline assumption that an outsider's primary motivation to join the WTO is to achieve improved market access to foreign economies, I argued that its economic power coupled with the multilateral reduction of trade barriers for its goods increases international competition of manufactured goods at two levels. First, old members' import-competing industries fear the influx of cheap products with tariff reductions in the course of a new member's accession. In the tradition of the political economy of trade and protection, redistributive conflicts are theorized to emerge in accession negotiations between the applicant's delegates and those member governments sensitive to political pressures of losing domestic import-competitors.

Chapter 4 explains how negotiating governments are caught between the dilemma of negotiating market access for their export-oriented corporations, while simultaneously granting minimum protection to losing import-competitors. I argue that the optimal trade policy tool for solving this political support trade off is to apply antidumping measures on causal goods and – at the same time – to promote the candidate's accession and negotiate improved market access for exporters. This subtle form of contingent protection hence minimizes domestic opposition against more general liberalization measures, enabling governments to support WTO enlargement. As a consequence, contingent protection additionally solves intra-organizational conflicts between those governments unconditionally favouring enlargement, and those facing domestic constraints.

Empirical observations reveal that China has evolved into the world's primary antidumping target during its WTO accession process. Regression results imply that the majority of the theoretically derived impact factors influences the levels of contingent protection old members' specific industries receive. The industry-specific number of antidumping measures on Chinese goods is for instance positively related to the import penetration ratio, to the respective industry's size, its labour intensity and its fear of future Chinese retaliation.

The interaction of these results with theoretic considerations provides confidence that these factors causally impact the level of contingent protection, especially because the influence is proven to increase over time towards China's accession and thereafter. This finally implies that governments do in fact replace traditional trade barriers against China, given by its historical WTO outsider status, by anti-dumping measures in the face of prospective WTO enlargement.

In broader terms, Chapter 4 demonstrated that domestic fears of increasing competition caused by a powerful new WTO member do not pose an insolvable problem to governments. Rather, the protectionist bias and the legal loopholes in WTO antidumping rules supply them with an efficient and legal regulative tool to keep the inflow of goods under control. Hence, satisfying minor special interests with contingent protection can help to pursue broader liberalization strategies. In the case of WTO enlargement, this means that old members' governments can cope with an increase of import-competition caused by the accession of a new member, although not without limiting the new member's benefits from joining the trade-agreement.

Governments are however powerless if economically powerful candidates do not only challenge import-competitors, but, second, also export-oriented corporations on third-markets. Chapter 5 theoretically sketches the emergence and consequences of third-market competition, which arise when WTO candidates' exporters receive equal market access to old members' trading partners. I argue that since third-market competition emerges abroad as a result of other countries' trade liberalization with the applicant country, governments have no alternative but to oppose its membership, which significantly delays the accession process. In other words, excluding powerful prospective new members from the WTO is the most efficient way to prolong quota rents for own exporters.

Surprisingly, the origins and effects of third-market competition have attracted only little scholarly attention – in the specific WTO enlargement literature as well as in more general liberalization theories. Especially approaches based on specific-factors assumptions commonly model export-oriented industries as winners of free-trade agreements. This is only valid if liberalization measures of the agreement are bilateral and reciprocal. Liberalization negotiations of the WTO accession process are bilateral in nature, but multilateral in effect. It is especially the step of multilateralization which results for instance in equal market access conditions for China and Mexico to the USA: bilaterally negotiated between Mexico and the USA, but with its accession also valid for China. As a result, Chinese and Mexican exporters compete in the USA for market shares. The less competitive exporters face income losses.

Chapter 5 demonstrates that this simple logic has far reaching consequences for especially newly industrialized accession candidates to the WTO because protectionist demands arising from increased third-market competition do not follow the traditional North-South divide of trade conflicts and protectionism. Instead, theoretical considerations expect countries similarly endowed as the applicant to be especially affected by income losses for exporters. That is, newly industrialized and developing economies with a congruent range of export specializations from chemicals over textiles and clothing to more advanced consumer electronics and computer parts do not only face increased protectionist responses from high-income industrialized countries on the basis of import-competition, but also from similarly endowed and neighbouring countries for the motives of third-market competition. This implies that the more diverse the export structure and the higher the output of exports of an applicant is, the more opposition it faces from a heterogeneous set of countries in the accession negotiations.

The case study delineating China's accession process partly supports the expectations that countries with larger fractions of exporters losing from China's accession than those winning from extra access to the Chinese economy have been relatively reluctant negotiators. This is especially true for more advanced countries competing for technical products, which are additionally not much protected through preferential access agreements and if their trade volume to China is small. Mexico has proven to be the most crucial case, delaying accession by one year after critical issues with the EU, the USA and all other main negotiators had been settled. Other resistant governments were those of India, Malaysia, Thailand and Poland. However, the case study design also reveals the importance of delay factors highlighted in previous research and encounters significant difficulties of isolating the intended delay effect from structural and institutional reasons for the 15 year long accession process.

The joined results of Chapters 4 and 5 reveal the magnitude of opposition applicant countries face in accession negotiation as a function of the redistributive conflicts they cause. Thus, the more an applicant increases the level of competition, the more will other members try to protect their losing industries. Increasing protectionist responses in the form of antidumping thereby derogate candidates' gains from trade and hence their benefits from WTO membership. Besides such indirect limitations of membership rights, Chapter 5 highlighted overt discrimination – expressed by the delay of accession as a function of increasing competition on third-markets. Although these mechanisms have been illustrated in the case of China's accession, they also apply to other free-trade enlargement procedures. However, due to the fact that the accession problems are a function of economic power, the mechanisms are less visible in accessions of countries with lower trade volumes compared to China.

Today, China's WTO membership heads towards its fifth anniversary, enabling it to likewise initiate antidumping measures, or to file complaints of unfair foreign trade policies to the dispute settlement body. Consequentially, Chapter 6 rounds off the analysis by exploring if China evolved into a cooperative WTO member, or if it utilizes its newly won membership rights to retaliate upon contra-integrationist members. The description of China's antidumping practices and trade dispute involvement reveals that, so far, China has chosen to strike a balance of active participation within the WTO without directly provoking other members. It nevertheless seems likely that especially China's future dispute settlement participation will increase with its economic growth and the phasing out of remaining membership transition regulations.

7.2 Generalizability of Results and Outlook

Due to its economic significance, China is a crucial case among all WTO accessions since 1995. The causal factor for the emergence of conflicts in its accession negotiations is – in most general terms – the contestation of international manufactures. On an aggregated level, it is the accelerated growth, volume and competitiveness of industrial output which triggered opposition to its WTO membership on larger a scale. No other WTO applicant comes close to China's economic power. Nevertheless, the mechanisms mapped out and analyzed within this book for the Chinese case, are also valid for the accession of other newly industrialized and transition economies as well.

From a theoretical point of view, there is no difference if Chinese exporters of computer parts or for instance Lithuanian exporters of TV picture tubes challenge other similar exporters on third-markets. Empirically however, the cumulated competition caused by Lithuanian exporters is not sufficient to trigger overt opposition against Lithuania's WTO accession. Thus, while the theoretical considerations generally apply to other WTO accessions as well, it requires candidates' pronounced economic power to make them *observable*.

From this perspective, future research also needs to be conducted for the analysis of conflicts in current WTO negotiations. The most prominent WTO non-members are The Russian Federation, Ukraine and Vietnam. While the former two are still in the midst of bilateral negotiations, Vietnam seems to be close to accession with two remaining bilateral agreements to be reached. Although it is a significantly smaller economy than China, a number of analogies exist between the two accessions processes.

First, the working party to the accession of Vietnam was founded in January of 1995, meaning that negotiations started almost 13 years ago. Keeping in mind that two final agreements need to be reached before bilaterals can be multilateralized for Vietnam's tariff schedules, it seems likely that in end, Vietnam's accession process will have taken similarly long as China's 15 years lasting odyssey to the WTO. Second, the overall interest in Vietnam's membership conditions is comparable to the Chinese case: The working party to the accession of Vietnam is considerably large in size (63 members) and similarly composed of mostly newly industrialized and transition economies from different regions. Third, while still only accounting for 0.30 % (in 2004) of world exports, Vietnam's industrial growth of the past years gives rise to suspicion that this interest is not exclusively rooted in its domestic tariff concessions, but also in potentially competition on third-markets. Fourth and finally, now that Vietnam is known to be in the final negotiation phase, antidumping measures levied on Vietnamese goods drastically increased.[33]

The working party to the accession of Russia was established in June 1993, but unlike Vietnam, its membership remains a distant prospect. Of 58 interested working party members, 29 had finalized bilateral negotiations by April 2005. As commonly known, Russia's export structure is completely different from that of China. Only one third of exports are manufactures, in contrast to 60 % fuels and mining products. The lack of highly competitive industries reduces the probability that ongoing negotiations are significantly delayed due to fear of third-market competition in manufactured goods.[34]

Factors impacting Russia's and other current applicants' pace of accessions are still unexplored. Further research is needed to determine if competitive pressures for old members also triggers political conflicts in these countries' membership negotiations, or if stumbling blocs arise from alternative explanations, e.g. economic reform reluctance and institutional features of the WTO accession procedure. Unfortunately, analyses of current accession processes are on hold until sufficient information about the negotiation phase is published. Since WTO enlargement is a politically sensitive subject, most information is classified up to the day of accession and some, e.g. bilateral negotiation protocols, also thereafter. This clearly complicates predictions about the accession timing of candidates and the explanation of political conflict in accession negotiations of new members, such as the People's Republic of China.

However, future research on multilateral free-trade and WTO enlargement must focus on the role of old members' intended protectionism and opposition to potential new members. This work demonstrates that WTO enlargement is not only lengthy and burdensome because of newly industrialized and transition countries' incapability to reform and adjust to WTO rules, but because old members deliberately exclude them from the trade club for protectionist motives when the candidate displays a significant trade volume. This leads to the paradox situation that reform-willing and economic powerful countries profiting most from WTO

---

[33] For further information on Vietnam's accession process please consult http://www.wto.org/English/thewto_e/acc_e/a1_vietnam_e.htm.

[34] For further information on Russia's accession process please consult http://www.wto.org/English/thewto_e/acc_e/a1_russie_e.htm.

membership face lengthy and conflictual accession negotiations, while small and economically insignificant countries depending less on the benefits offered by the WTO can join without causing a stir.

8 APPENDIX

The following table contains the full negative binomial model specifications including unit dummies for countries and industries, which are excluded from the tables in Chapter 4 for the sake of clarity. Models 1 through model 4 are identical with earlier estimations. However, the multicollinearity of those unit dummies which always display zero outcomes on the dependent variable, that is, those industries or countries which never apply AD measures, causes inflated standard errors. Model 5 solves this problem by excluding the collinear units with a reduced sample, which bisects the observations compared to the original Model one. This proceeding simply serves as a test of robustness: although almost half of the observations dropped, coefficients and standard errors remain identical. Consequentially, multicollinearity of the dummy variables does not impact the results and can be neglected. The full model specification reveals the influential countries and industries as discussed in Section 4.2.2.

Table 8.1 Negative Binomial Specification Including Country and Industry Dummies

x-Variables (y=AD)	Model 1	Model 2	Model 3	Model 4	Model 5
Rel.Ind.Size	9.317***	12.057***	11.712***	7.868***	9.316***
	(2.849)	(2.772)	(2.667)	(2.038)	(2.849)
Ind.Sim.	-0.398	-0.313	-0.235	-0.273	-0.398
	(0.248)	(0.248)	(0.238)	(0.239)	(0.248)
Imp.Pen.Ratio	4.345**	5.168**	4.240**		4.345**
	(2.027)	(2.012)	(1.914)		(2.027)
Exp.ToChina	-3.090**	-2.756**			-3.090**
	(1.302)	(1.286)			(1.302)
GDP/Capita	-0.239***				-0.239***
	(0.069)				(0.069)
early:1995-1997	0.984***	0.516*	0.523*	0.608**	0.984***
	(0.346)	0.305)	(0.294)	(0.293)	(0.346)
final:1998-2000	2.369***	1.447***	1.391***	1.475***	2.369***
	(0.416)	(0.291)	(0.275)	(0.273)	(0.416)
post:2001-2003	2.528***	1.319***	1.165***	1.305***	2.528***
	(0.479)	(0.297)	(0.277)	(0.271)	(0.479)
01-Agriculture	2.186**	2.023**	1.753**	1.598*	2.186**
	(0.862)	(0.863)	(0.836)	(0.833)	(0.862)
10-Coal&Mining	1.611	1.566	1.477	0.884	1.611
	(1.092)	(1.099)	(1.029)	(1.006)	(1.092)
14-Quarrying	1.829**	1.855**	1.755**	1.425*	1.829**
	(0.854)	(0.855)	(0.846)	(0.830)	(0.854)
15-Food	0.062	-0.138	-0.315	-0.464	0.062
	(1.073)	(1.073)	(1.058)	(1.056)	(1.073)
16-Tobacco	-14.921	-13.750	-14.032	-15.617	

Table 8.1 continued

x-Variables (y=AD)	Model 1	Model 2	Model 3	Model 4	Model 5
	(5168.241)	(3603.768)	(4445.768)	(3654.316)	
17-Textiles	1.918**	1.830**	1.901**	1.979**	1.918**
	(0.830)	(0.831)	(0.817)	(0.816)	(0.830)
18-Apparel	-0.548	-0.530	-0.677	-0.636	-0.547
	(1.283)	(1.287)	(1.270)	(1.269)	(1.283)
19-Leath.&Footwear	2.522***	2.494***	2.520***	2.593***	2.522***
	(0.817)	(0.819)	(0.802)	(0.799)	(0.817)
20-Wood	-0.056	0.022	-0.093	-0.508	-0.056
	(1.284)	(1.284)	(1.276)	(1.261)	(1.284)
21-Paper	1.328	1.367	1.247	0.837	1.328
	(0.898)	(0.897)	(0.885)	(0.864)	(0.898)
23-Coke&Petr.	-16.733	-15.609	-15.779	-15.813	
	(4174.541)	(2405.416)	(2482.080)	(2018.302)	
24-Chemicals	3.315***	3.041***	2.840***	3.039***	3.315***
	(0.830)	(0.826)	(0.804)	(0.799)	(0.830)
25-Rubber&Plastic	1.843**	1.832**	1.794	1.473*	1.843**
	(0.891)	(0.893)	(0.877)	(0.863)	(0.891)
26-Minerals	1.650*	1.648*	1.532*	1.442*	1.650*
	(0.844)	(0.846)	(0.835)	(0.832)	(0.844)
27-BasicMetals	2.800***	2.604***	2.353***	2.251***	2.800***
	(0.822)	(0.820)	(0.791)	(0.788)	(0.822)
28-Fabri.Metals	2.498***	2.296***	2.306***	2.447***	2.498***
	(0.828)	(0.827)	(0.812)	(0.808)	(0.828)
29-Machinery	3.016***	2.853***	2.728***	2.958***	3.016***
	(0.818)	(0.817)	(0.800)	(0.793)	(0.818)
31-Electr.Apparatus	1.238	1.124	1.087	1.273	1.238
	(0.848)	(0.848)	(0.839)	(0.834)	(0.848)
32-Radio&TV	-0.014	-0.147	-0.098	0.068	-0.014
	(0.968)	(0.970)	(0.966)	(0.961)	(0.968)
33-Prec.Instruments	-0.911	-0.969	0.141	0.112	-0.911
	(1.276)	(1.292)	(0.980)	(0.976)	(1.276)
34-MotorVehicles	1.864**	1.743**	1.773**	1.632**	1.864**
	(0.863)	(0.863)	(0.834)	(0.830)	(0.863)
35-Trans.Equipment	0.330	0.374	-0.190	-0.872	0.330
	(1.322)	(1.325)	(1.304)	(1.266)	(1.322)
36-Furniture	-0.785	-1.021	-0.958	-1.057	-0.785
	(1.298)	(1.330)	(1.296)	(1.282)	(1.298)
ARG	4.057***	2.956***	3.187***	3.002***	4.057***
	(1.128)	(1.076)	(1.062)	(1.059)	(1.128)
AUS	6.312***	1.774	1.805	1.930*	6.312***
	(1.732)	(1.115)	(1.115)	(1.116)	(1.732)
BOL	-19.303	-17.360	-16.413	-16.621	
	(11187.713)	(7541.582)	(4131.047)	(3752.174)	
BRA	3.508***	3.360***	3.290***	3.026***	3.508***
	(1.078)	(1.073)	(1.070)	(1.065)	(1.078)
CAN	7.107***	2.327**	2.358**	2.538**	7.107***
	(1.767)	(1.078)	(1.078)	(1.078)	(1.767)

Table 8.1 continued

x-Variables (y=AD)	Model 1	Model 2	Model 3	Model 4	Model 5
CHL	-17.804	-17.206)	-17.124	-16.773	
	(8059.541)	(4352.146)	(4643.895)	(3741.377)	
CHLI	-12.801	-16.849	-17.263	-16.863	
	(6611.533)	(3577.769)	(4520.443)	(3701.916)	
COL	-18.321	-16.940	-16.537	-16.468	
	(9773.608)	(5465.030)	(4877.803)	(3983.013)	
CRI	-18.332	-17.549	-17.327	-17.264	
	(13477.110)	(7131.194)	(4870.945)	(3924.589)	
CZE	-16.045	-16.610	-16.866	-16.577	
	(6843.021)	(3731.140)	(4573.072)	(3739.102)	
ECU	-17.943	-15.536	-15.515	-15.847	
	(9970.839)	(5549.187)	(4183.469)	(3649.526)	
EGY	-0.331	0.568	0.464	0.251	-0.331
	(1.506)	(1.482)	(1.445)	(1.442)	(1.506)
EUEX	8.014***	3.501***	3.320***	3.672***	8.014***
	(1.697)	(1.059)	(1.055)	(1.047)	(1.697)
GTM	-19.537	-17.528	-17.065	-17.134	
	(28662.404)	(14633.936)	(5052.653)	(4066.119)	
HUN	-16.514	-16.554	-16.582	-16.475	
	(6833.476)	(3773.784)	(4384.951)	(3687.168)	
IDN	-18.006	-16.004	-16.505	-16.175	
	(5856.903)	(3255.215)	(4240.935)	(3506.362)	
IND	2.910***	3.973***	4.035***	3.832***	2.910***
	(1.095)	(1.051)	(1.051)	(1.047)	(1.095)
ISR	3.072*	0.097	0.224	0.031	3.072*
	(1.694)	(1.447)	(1.443)	(1.440)	(1.694)
JPN	-13.330	-16.697	-17.438	-16.643	
	(6383.309)	(3299.374)	(4369.551)	(3529.089)	
KOR	3.501***	1.456	1.225	1.498	3.501***
	(1.282)	(1.127)	(1.120)	(1.116)	(1.282)
LTU	-16.491	-15.742	-15.585	-16.135	
	(8281.752)	(5081.583)	(4562.869)	(4086.169)	
LVA	-17.371	-15.848	-15.324	-16.039	
	(15246.473)	(8079.023)	(4390.608)	(3986.836)	
MAR	-18.864	-16.952	-16.626	-16.564	
	(9929.202)	(5511.805)	(4505.882)	(3683.123)	
MEX	3.698***	3.240***	3.463***	3.377***	3.698***
	(1.073)	(1.060)	(1.049)	(1.050)	(1.073)
MYS	-17.219	-16.471	-17.046	-16.513	
	(6536.199)	(3352.684)	(4371.301)	(3564.886)	
NOR	-11.090	-16.260	-16.591	-16.386	
	(6185.210)	(3446.120)	(4402.806)	(3621.674)	
NZL	3.265**	0.036	0.225	0.246	3.265**
	(1.579)	(1.262)	(1.258)	(1.259)	(1.579)
PAK	-19.278	-16.927	-16.917	-16.616	
	(7840.371)	(4166.432)	(4808.773)	(3811.361)	
PAN	-14.187	-14.292	-13.437	-14.338	

Table 8.1 continued

x-Variables (y=AD)	Model 1	Model 2	Model 3	Model 4	Model 5
	(3177.204)	(3727.599)	(1739.310)	(1975.969)	
PER	1.416	1.937	2.335**	2.054*	1.416
	(1.195)	(1.180)	(1.097)	(1.091)	(1.195)
PHL	0.014	0.617	0.754	0.676	0.014
	(1.274)	(1.258)	(1.254)	(1.256)	(1.274)
POL	1.142	0.420	0.637	0.554	1.142
	(1.287)	(1.267)	(1.257)	(1.257)	(1.287)
ROM	-17.485	-16.384	-16.413	-16.408	
	(6318.235)	(4139.869)	(4441.204)	(3695.821)	
SGP	-13.990	-16.415	-17.071	-16.410	
	(6094.034)	(3182.950)	(4085.456)	(3416.272)	
SLV	-20.098	-18.166	-17.266	-17.220	
	(18930.012)	(9533.901)	(4960.066)	(3984.152)	
SVK	-16.987	-16.923	-16.549	-16.590	
	(8411.085)	(4738.020)	(4325.157)	(3731.344)	
SVN	-16.525	-17.576	-17.391	-17.176	
	(9272.616)	(4873.349)	(4768.776)	(3804.695)	
TUN	-18.885	-17.547	-17.087	-16.957	
	(12443.006)	(6825.422)	(4775.803)	(3801.697)	
TUR	1.921*	2.075*	2.334**	2.227**	1.921*
	(1.096)	(1.092)	(1.083)	(1.082)	(1.096)
URY	-17.865	-17.219	-16.733	-16.730	
	(8952.763)	(5324.907)	(4194.673)	(3589.985)	
USA	10.693***	4.646***	4.420***	4.774***	10.693***
	(2.079)	(1.072)	(1.066)	(1.058)	(2.079)
VEN	1.633	1.964	2.217**	1.795	1.633
	(1.211)	(1.213)	(1.129)	(1.114)	(1.211)
ZAF	4.192***	3.520***	3.739***	3.555***	4.192***
	(1.082)	(1.058)	(1.054)	(1.051)	(1.082)
Constant	-15.159***	-18.531***	-18.888	-13.652***	-15.158***
	(3.421)	(3.315)	(3.191)	(2.133)	(3.421)
Obs	2512	2512	3637	3637	1294
Pseudo R^2	0.354	0.346	0.374	0.371	0.249

Note: Figures are ML estimates with standard errors in parentheses, ***, **, and * denote z-statistics at the 99 %, 95 %, and 90 % confidence level, respectively.

To further check of robustness, Table 8.2 contains the results of the random effects panel estimation. Please note that the random effect specification has not been chosen as a baseline model since the assumption of normal distributed and random unit effects necessary for random effects models is violated per definition in the antidumping case: Some industries and countries, that is, the 'units' are expected to exert stronger impacts than others. The output is nevertheless consistent with the main results. Relative industry size, the import penetration ratio and export shares are positively and statistically significant related to the probability of increased antidumping practices against China. Over and above, the random effects specification enables the inclusion of the political power variable *district magnitude,* which is found not to be robustly significant. *District magnitude* is an almost time invariant variable which perfectly correlates with the units in the fixed effects specification (Pluemper and Troeger 2004), and is therefore included in this random panel model.

The theoretical argument that policy-makers in relatively small electorate districts react more sensitively to the protectionist demands of special industries and bring these into the legislative process with the result of protection-biased AD authorities cannot be supported. Traditionally, this variable has been applied to assess its *direct* impact on protectionist outcomes, that is, cases where the policy maker subject to lobbying can directly grant protection. Antidumping protection is however administered, that is, policy-makers can only impact the design of AD institutions, but not the direct outcome. Therefore, *district magnitude* is not suitable to assess the impact of protectionist demands on AD protection.

Table 8.2 Negative Binomial Random Effects Panel Specification

Variable	Model 1	Model 2	Model 3	Model 4
DistrictMagnitude	-0.010	-0.010	-0.011*	-0.018**
	0.007	0.006	0.006	0.007
RelativeIndustrySize	7.749***	7.324***	8.787***	2.653
	2.224	2.210	2.015	1.643
IndustrySimilarity	0.101	0.122	0.129	0.191
	0.218	0.219	0.208	0.218
ImportPenetrationRatio	5.705***	4.595***	8.141***	
	1.606	1.504	1.334	
ExportsToChina	2.775***	2.163**		
	1.068	1.023		
GDPPerCapita	-0.031**			
	0.015			
early:1995-1997	0.301	0.272	0.273	0.555**
	0.282	0.279	0.270	0.276
final:1998-2000	0.959***	0.858***	0.934***	1.220***
	0.260	0.255	0.244	0.250
post:2001-2003	0.797***	0.700***	0.715***	1.112***
	0.266	0.261	0.250	0.253
Constant	-10.490***	-9.741***	-11.766***	-2.662**
	2.278	2.232	2.097	1.357
Observations	2250	2250	3194	3194

Note: Figures are ML estimates with standard errors in parentheses, ***, **, and * denote *z*-statistics at the 99 %, 95 %, and 90 % confidence level, respectively.

Table 8.3　Sample Industries

ISIC 2-Digit	Industry Name
01	Agriculture, hunting and related service activities
10	Mining of coal and lignite; extraction of peat
14	Other mining and quarrying
15	Manufacture of food products and beverages
16	Manufacture of tobacco products
17	Manufacture of textiles
18	Manufacture of wearing apparel; dressing and dyeing of fur
19	Tanning and dressing of leather; manufacture of luggage, handbags, saddlery, harness and footwear
20	Manufacture of wood and of products of wood and cork, except furniture; manufacture of articles of straw and plaiting materials
21	Manufacture of paper and paper products
23	Manufacture of coke, refined petroleum products and nuclear fuel
24	Manufacture of chemicals and chemical products
25	Manufacture of rubber and plastics products
26	Manufacture of other non-metallic mineral products
27	Manufacture of basic metals
28	Manufacture of fabricated metal products, except machinery and equipment
29	Manufacture of machinery and equipment n.e.c.
30	Manufacture of office, accounting and computing machinery
31	Manufacture of electrical machinery and apparatus n.e.c.
32	Manufacture of radio, television and communication equipment and apparatus
33	Manufacture of medical, precision and optical instruments, watches and clocks
34	Manufacture of motor vehicles, trailers and semi-trailers
35	Manufacture of other transport equipment
36	Manufacture of furniture; manufacturing n.e.c.

Table 8.4 Sample Countries

ARG	Argentina	MYS	Malaysia
AUS	Australia	NEX	Mexico
BOL	Bolivia	MAR	Morocco
BRA	Brazil	NZL	New Zealand
CAN	Canada	NOR	Norway
CHL	Chile	PAK	Pakistan
COL	Colombia	PAN	Panama
CRI	Costa Rica	PER	Peru
CZE	Czech Republic	PHL	Philippines
ECU	Ecuador	POL	Poland
EGY	Egypt	ROM	Romania
SLV	El Salvador	SGP	Singapore
EU	European Union	SVK	Slovakia
GTM	Guatemala	SVN	Slovenia
HUN	Hungary	ZAF	South Africa
IND	India	CHLI	Switzerland Liechtenstein
IDN	Indonesia	THA	Thailand
ISR	Israel	TUN	Tunisia
JPN	Japan	TUR	Turkey
KOR	Republic of Korea	URY	Uruguay
LVA	Latvia	USA	USA
LTU	Lithuania	VEN	Venezuela

9 BIBLIOGRAPHY

Alt, James E., and Gilligan Michael. 1994. The Political Economy of Trading States: Factor Specifity, Collective Action Problems and Domestic Political Institutions. *Journal of Political Philosophy* 2 (2):165-192.

Alt, James E., Jeffry Frieden, Michael J. Gilligan, Dani Rodrik, and Ronald Rogowski. 1996. The Political Economy of International Trade. Comparative Political Studies 29 (6):689-717.

Anderson, Kym.1997. On the Complexities of China's WTO Accession. The World Economy 20 (6): 749-772.

Associated Press Online. April 13th, 2000. China, Malaysia Sign WTO Deal. Accessible at http://www.lexisnexis.com/

Bagwell, Kyle, and Robert W. Staiger. 1996. Reciprocal Trade Liberalization. NBER Working Paper 5488.

Bagwell, Kyle, and Robert W. Staiger. 1997. Reciprocity, Non-Discrimination and Preferential Agreements in the Multilateral Trading System. NBER Working Paper 5932.

Balassa, Bela. 1965. Trade Liberalization and Revealed Comparative Advantage. Manchester School of Economic and Social Studies 33 (2): 99-123.

Baldwin, Robert E. 1998. Imposing Multilateral Discipline on Administered Protection. In The WTO as an International Organization, edited by A. O. Krueger. Chicago: The University of Chicago Press.

Banks, Gary. 1993. The Antidumping Experience of a GATT-Fearing Country. In Antidumping. How It Works and Who Gets Hurt, edited by J. M. Finger. Ann Arbor: The University of Michigan Press.

BBC Worldwide Monitoring. December 1st, 1999. China hopes to make progress on WTO entry at Seattle meeting. Accessible at http://www.lexisnexis.com/

Beijing Review. November 1999. Chronology of China's Bid for WTO Accession. http://www.china.org.cn/Beijing-Review/Beijing/BeijingReview/99Nov/bjr99-48e-8.html, last consulted on September 12, 2005

Blonigen, Bruce A., and Chad P. Bown. 2001. Antidumping and Retaliation Threats. NBER Working Paper Series 8576.

Blonigen, Bruce A., and Thomas J. Prusa. 2001. Antidumping. NBER Working Paper 8398.

Bond, Eric, Stephen Ching, and Edwin L. C. Lai. 2000. Accession Rules and Trade Agreements: The Case of the WTO. *Econometric Society World Congress 2000 Working Paper* 1626.

Bond, Eric, Stephen Ching, and Edwin L. C. Lai. 2003. Game-Theoretic Analysis of China's WTO Accession. *Pacific Economic Review* 8 (2):117-126.

Bourgeois, Jaques H., and Patrick A. Messerlin. 1998. The European Community's Experience. In Brookings Trade Forum 1998, edited by R. Z. Lawrence. Washington, D.C.: Brookings Institution Press.

Bown, Chad P. 2005. Participation in WTO Dispute Settlement: Complaints, Interested Parties, and Free Riders. The World Bank Economic Review 19 (2):287-310.

Bridges Weekly Trade News Digest. February 22nd, 2000. WTO Accessions Update: China and the Middle East. http://www.newsbulletin.org/getbuletin.cfm?browse=1&Issue_ID=1700& Bulletin_ID=14&SID=#WTO%20Accessions%20Update%3A%20China%20and%20the%20Middle%20East, last consulted on April 7, 2006

Broude, Tomer. 1998. Accession to the WTO. Current Issues in the Arab World. Journal of World Trade 32 (6): 147-166.

Busch, Marc L., and Eric Reinhardt. 2006. Three is a Crowd: Third Parties and WTO Dispute Settlement. Working Paper, accessible at http://userwww.service.emory.edu/~erein/research/3p.pdf, last consulted on April 22nd, 2006.

Cass, Deborah Z., Brett G. Williams, and George Barker. 2003. Introduction: China and the reshaping of the World Trade Organization. in D. Z. Cass, B. G. Williams and G. Barker (eds) China and the World Trading System. Entering the New Millennium, pp. 1-18. Cambridge: Cambridge University Press.

Conybeare, John A. C. 1991. Voting for Protection: An Electoral Model of Tariff Policy. International Organization 45 (1): 57-81.

Dickson, Ian. 2003. China's interest in the World Trade Organization's deregulation of international textiles trade. In China and the World Trading System. Entering the New Millenium, edited by D. Z. Cass, B. G. Williams and G. Barker. Cambridge: Cambridge University Press.

Dutz, Mark. 1998. Economic Impact of Canadian Antidumping Law. In Brooking Trade Forum 1998, edited by R. Z. Lawrence. Washington, D.C.: Brookings Institution Press.

Ethier, Wilfred J. 2004. Political Externalities, Nondiscrimination, and a Multilateral World. Review of International Economics 12 (3): 303-320.

European Union External Relations. 2005a. The Euro - Mediterranean Partnership.
http://europa.eu.int/comm/external_relations/euromed/med_ass_agreemnt s.htm, last consulted on July 22, 2005.

European Union Press Releases. 2005b. EU – China textile agreement 10 June 2005.
http://www.europa.eu.int/rapid/pressReleasesAction.do?reference=MEMO/05/201&format=HTML&aged=0&language=en&guiLanguage=en, last consulted on August 12, 2005.

Evans, Carolyn L., and James Harrigan. 2004. Tight Clothing: How the MFA Affects Asian Apparel Exports. NBER Working Paper 10250.

Eymann, Angelika, and Ludger Schuknecht. 1993. Antidumping Enforcement in the European Community. In Antidumping. How it Works and Who Gets Hurt, edited by J. M. Finger. Ann Arbor: The University of Michigan Press.

Fearon, James D. 1998. Bargaining, Enforcement, and International Cooperation. International Organization 52 (2):269-305.

Feaver, Donald, and Kenneth Wilson. 2004. The Political Economy of Contingent Protection. The International Trade Journal 18 (3):199-237.

Federick, Shane, George Loewenstein, and Ted O'Donoghue. 2002. Time Discounting and Time Preferences: A Critical Review. Journal of Economic Literature 40:351-401.

Feenstra, R.C., and J.N. Bhagwati. 1982. Tariff seeking and the efficient tariff, in J. N. Bhagwati (ed) Import competition and response, pp. 245-262. Chicago: University of Chicago Press.

Fewsmith, Joseph. 1999. China and the WTO: The Politics Behind the Agreement. The National Bureau of Asian Research 10 (5): Essay 2.

Financial Times January 10, 2001. China puts Mexican trade in the line of fire: Nafta's export advantages will be lost once Beijing wins the battle for WTO entry. Page 13.

Financial Times July 21, 2001. China close to finalising WTO entry negotiations. Page 7.

Financial Times July 3, 2001. WTO plans al-out push for China accession. Page 10.

Financial Times May 4, 2005. Fifteen poorest countries lobby US to give garment preferences. Page 9.

Financial Times. December 10, 2001. Enter the dragon: Economic uncertainties raised by China's accession to the WTO are likely to put pressure on international trade relations for years to come. Page 22.

Findlay, R., and S. Wellisz. 1982. Endogenous Tarifs, the Political Economy Trade Restrictions, and Welfare. in J. N. Bhagwati (ed) Import competition and response, pp. 223-244. Chicago: University of Chicago Press.

Finger, J. Michael. 2002. Safeguards: Making Sense of GATT/WTO Provisions Allowing for Import Restrictions. In Development, Trade, and the WTO, edited by B. Hoekman, A. Mattoo and P. English. Washington, D.C.: The World Bank.

Finger, J.M. 1993. Antidumping. How it Works and Who Gets Hurt. Ann Arbor: University of Michigan Press.

Finger, J.M., H.K. Hall, and D.R. Nelson. 1982. The political economy of administered protection. American Economic Review 72 (3):452-466.

Finger, Michael J., Ulrich Reincke, and Adriana Castro. 2002. Market Access Bargaining in the Uruguay Round: How Tightly Does Reciprocity Constrain? in J. Bhagwati (ed) Going Alone. The Case for Relaxed Reciprocity in Freeing Trade, pp. 111-136. Cambridge: MIT Press.

GAO, United States General Accounting Office 2002. Analysis of China's Commitments to Other Members. Report GAO-03-4. www.gao.gov/cgi-bin/getrpt?GAO-03-4, last consulted on July 22. 2005.

Gertler, Jeffrey L. 2003. China's WTO accession - the final countdown, in D. Z. Cass, B. G. Williams and G. Barker (eds) China and the World Trading System. Entering the New Millennium, pp. 55-67. Cambridge: Cambridge University Press.

Golder, Matt. 2004. Democratic Electoral Systems Around the World. Electoral Studies 24:103-121.

Grossman, G, and E. Helpman. 2001. Special Interest Politics. Campridge: MIT Press.

Grossman, G.M., and E. Helpman. 1994. Protection for Sale. American Economic Review 84: 833-850.

Hausmann, Ricardo, Jason Hwang, and Dani Rodrik. 2005. What You Export Matters NBER Working Paper 11905.

Hillman, Arye L. 1989. The Political Economy of Protection. Chur: Harwood Academic Publishers.

Hillman, Arye L. 2003. Trade Liberalization and Globalization: A Survey. CEPR Discussion Paper Series 3845.

Hillman, Arye L., and P. Moser. 1996. Trade Liberalization as Politically Opti mal Exchange of Market Access, in M. Canzoneri, W. J. Ethier and V. Grilli (eds) The new Transatlantic Economy, pp. 295-312. Cambridge: Cambridge University Press.

Hoekman, Bernard M., and Michel M. Kostecki. 2001. The Political Economy of the World Trading System. Oxford: Oxford University Press.

Ianchovichina, Elena, and Terrie Walmsley. 2005. Impact of China's WTO Accession on East Asia. Contemporary Economic Policy 23 (2):261-277.

Ianchovichina, Elena, and Terrie Walmsley. 2005. Impact of China's WTO Accession on East Asia. Contemporary Economic Policy 23 (2): 261-277.

Ianchovichina, Elena, and Will Martin. 2001. Trade Liberalization in China's Accession to WTO. Journal of Economic Integration 16 (4):421-445.

Ianchovichina, Elena, and Will Martin. 2003. Economic Impacts of China's Accession to the WTO. World Bank Policy Research Working Paper No. 3053, World Bank, 2003.

ITC / United Nations Statistics Division. PC/TAS: Trade Analysis System On Personal Computer. SITC Rev. 3 1993 – 2002.

Ja Shin, Hyuan. 1998. Possible Instances of Predatory Pricing in Recent U.S. Antidumping Cases. In Brookings Trade Forum 1998, edited by R. Z. Lawrence. Washington, D.C.: The Brookings Institution Press.

Jackson, John H. 2003. The Impact of China's Accession on the WTO. In China and the World Trading System. Entering the New Millenium, edited by D. Z. Cass, B. G. Williams and G. Barker. Cambridge: Cambridge University Press.

Kennett, Maxine, Simon J. Evenett and Jonathan Gage. 2005. Evaluating WTO Accessions: Legal and Economic Perspectives. http://siteresources.worldbank.org/INTRANETTRADE/Resources/WBI-Training/EvaluatingWTOAccessions_partI.pdf, last consulted on September 12, 2005.

Knetter, Michael M., and Thomas J. Prusa. 2000. Macroeconomic Factors and Antidumping Filings: Evidence from Four Countries. NBER Working Paper Series 8010.

Krugman, Paul R. 1991. The Move Toward Free Trade Zones. Paper read at Policy Implications of Trade and Currency Zones, at Federal Reserve Bank of Kansas City.

Kufuor, Kofi Oteng. 1998. The Developing Countries and the Shaping of GATT/WTO Antidumping Law. Journal of World Trade 32(6):167-196.

Langhammer, Rolf J., and Matthias Lücke. 1999. WTO Accession Issues. Kiel Working Paper No. 905.

Lardy, Nicholas R. 2002. Integrating China into the global economy. Washington, D.C.: Brookings Institution Press.

Liang, Wei. 2002. China's WTO Negotiations Process and its Implications. Journal of Contemporary China 11 (33): 683-719.

Long, J. Scott, and Jeremy Freese. 2001. Regression Models for Categorical Dependent Variables Using Stata. Thousand Oaks: Sage.

Long, Yongtu 1997. Statement of H. E. Vice Minister Long Yongtu at the sixth Session of the Working Party Meeting on China's Accession to the WTO (December 5, 1997, Geneva). http://genevamissiontoun.fmprc.gov.cn/eng/13765.html, last consulted on September 12, 2005.

Magee, S.P., W.A. Brock, and L. Young. 1989. Black Hole Tariffs and Endogenous Policy Theory. Cambridge: Cambridge University Press.

Mallon, Glenda, and John Whalley. 2004. China's Post Accession WTO Stance. NBER Working Paper 10649.

Mansfield, Edward D., and Eric Reinhardt. 2003. Multilateral Determinants of Regionalism: The Efffects of GATT/WTO on the Formation of Preferential Trading Arrangements. International Organization 57 (4): 829-862.

Mansfield, Edward D., and Marc L. Busch. 1995. The Political Economy of Nontariff Barriers: A Cross-National Analysis. International Organization 49 (4):723-749.

Mayer, W. 1984. Endogenous Tariff Formation. American Economic Review 74: 970-985.

Merlo, Antonio, and Charles Wilson. 1995. A Stochastic Model of Sequential Bargaining with Complete Information. Ecomometrica 63 (2):371-399.

Messerlin, Patrick A. 2004. China in the World Trade Organization: Antidumping and Safeguards. The World Bank Economic Review 18 (1):105-130.

Messerlin, Patrick A., and P.K.M. Tharakan. 1999. The Question of Contingent Protection. The World Economy 22 (9):1251-1270.

Michalopoulos, Constantine. 1998. WTO Accession for Countries in Transition. World Bank Working Paper 1934.

Milner, Helen V. 1988. Resisting Protectionism. Princeton: Princeton University Press.

Milner, Helen V. 1999. The Political Economy of International Trade. Annual Review of Political Science 2:91-114.

Miranda, Jorge, Raúl A. Torres, and Mario Ruiz. 1998. The International Use of Antidumping: 1987-1997. Journal of World Trade 32 (5):5-71.

Niels, Gunnar, and Adriaan ten Kate. 2004. Anti-dumping Protection in a Liberalising Country: Mexico's Anti-dumping Policy and Practice. The World Economy 27 (7):967-983.

Ostry, Sylvia. 2003. WTO membership for China: to be and not to be - is that the answer? In China and the World Trading System. Entering the New Millennium, edited by D. Z. Cass, B. G. Williams and G. Barker. Cambridge: Cambridge University Press.

Panitchpakdi, Supachai, and Mark L. Clifford. 2002. China and the WTO. Changing China, Changing World Trade. Singapore: John Wiley & Son.

Pluemper, Thomas, and Vera E. Troeger. 2004. The Estimation of Time-Invariant Variables in Panel Analyses with Unit Fixed Effects. *SSRN Working Paper* http://ssrn.com/abstract=565904

Prusa, Thomas J. 2001. On the Spread and Impact of Antidumping. Canadian Journal of Economics 34 (3):591-611.

Prusa, Thomas J., and Susan Skeath. 2001. The Economic and Strategic Motives for Antidumping Filings. NBER Working Paper Series 8424.

Prusa, Thomas J., and Susan Skeath. 2004. Modern Commercial Policy: Managed Trade or Retaliation? In Handbook of International Trade, Vol. II, edited by E. K. Choi and J. Hartigan. London: Blackwell.

Putnam, Robert D. 1988. Diplomacy and Domestic Politics: The Logic of Two-Level Games. International Organization 42 (3):427-60.

Rhodes, Carolyn. 1989. Reciprocity in Trade: The Utility of a Bargaining Strategy. International Organization 43 (2): 273-299.

Ricart, Marc and Wei-Ling Chang. 2005. Latin America and China: Sino Amigos? More Latin American Winners than Losers Due to China's Developing Economy. Latin American Law and Business Report. January 2005. http://www.wtexecutive.com/cms/content.jsp?id=com.tms.cms.article.Arti cle_3a6f43cd-97cba9a0-1517e5e0-14d102a8, last consulted on April 7th, 2006

Rodrik, Dani. 1992. The Rush to Free Trade in the Developing World: Why So Late? Why Now? Will it Last? NBER Working Paper 3947.

Rodrik, Dani. 1995. Political Economy of Trade Policy. In Handbook of International Economics Vol. III, edited by G. Grossman and K. Rogoff. Amsterdam: Elsevier.

Rodrik, Dani. 2006. What's So Special About China's Exports? *NBER Working Paper* 11947.

Rogowski, Ronald. 1987. Political Cleavages and Changing Exposure to Trade. The American Political Science Review 81 (4):1121-1137.

Rogowski, Ronald. 1987. Trade and the Variety of Democratic Institutions. International Organization 41 (2):203-223.

Rumbaugh, Thomas, and Nicolas Blancher. 2004. China: International Trade and WTO Accession. IMF Working Paper WP/04/36.

Schneider, Christina J. 2005. Enlargement Negotiations and Distributional Conflicts. The Politics of Differentiated Membership in the European Union. Mimeo, University of Konstanz.

Shafaeddin, S.M. 2002. The Impact of China's Accession to WTO on the Exports of Developing Countries. UNCTAD Discussion Paper 160.

Song, Ligang. 2003. The state of the chinese economy - structural changes, impacts and implications. In China and the World Trading System. Entering the New Millennium, edited by D. Z. Cass, B. G. Williams and G. Barker. Cambridge: Cambridge University Press.

SUNS – South-North Development Monitor. 2000. Two More Sessions Planed On China Working Party. SUNS 4694, http://www.twnside.org.sg/title/sessions.htm, last consulted on September 12, 2005.

Sussangkarn, Chalongphob. 2004. The Emergence of China and ASEAN Revitalization. Annual Bank Conference on Development Economics Working Paper, http://wbln0018.worldbank.org/eurvp/web.nsf/Pages/Paper+by+Sussangk arn/$File/SUSSANGKARN.PDF, last consulted on September 12, 2005.

Tharakan, P.K.M. 1995. Political Economy and Contingent Protection. The Economic Journal 105 (433):1550-1564.

UNCTAD. 2001. WTO Accessions and Development Policies. UNCTAD/ DITC/TNCD/11. http://www.unctad.org/en/docs/ditctncd11_en.pdf, last consulted on February 12, 2006.

UNIDO. 2004. Industrial Statistics Database ISIC Rev. 3.

Van Long, N., and N. Vousden. 1991. Protectionist Responses and Declining Industries. Journal of International Economics 31: 87-103.

Walmsley, Terrie L., and Thomas W. Hertel. 2000. China's Accession to the WTO: Timing is Everything. GTAP Working Paper 13.

Wang, Zhi. 2000. The Impact of China's WTO Entry on the World Labour-intensive Export Market: A Recursive Dynamic CGE Analysis. World Economy 22 (3): 379-405.

Wang, Zhi. 2003. The impact of China's WTO accession on patterns of world trade. Journal of Policy Modeling 25: 1-41.

Willig, Robert D. 1998. Economic Effects of Antidumping Policy. In Brookings Trade Froum 1998, edited by R. Z. Lawrence. Washington, D.C.: Brookings Institution Press.

World Bank. 2004. World Development Indicators.

WTO. 1994. Agreement on Implementation of Article VI of the General Agreement on Tariffs and Trade' 1994.
http://www.wto.org/english/docs_e/legal_e/19-adp.pdf, last consulted on December 4th, 2005.

WTO. 1995. Accession to the World Trade Organization. WT/ACC/1.
http://docsonline.wto.org/DDFDocuments/t/WT/ACC/1.WPF,
last consulted on February 12, 2006

WTO. 2001. Accession of the People's Republic of China. WT/L/432.

WTO. 2004. Protocols of accession for new members since 1995, including commitments in goods and services',
http://www.wto.org/english/thewto_e/acc_e/completeacc_e.htm#ecu,
last consulted on July 22, 2005.

WTO. DS252. United States — Definitive Safeguard Measures on Imports of Certain Steel Products
http://www.wto.org/English/tratop_e/dispu_e/cases_e/ds252_e.htm,
last consulted on April 22nd, 2006

WTO. DS267. United States – Subsidies on Upland Cotton.
http://www.wto.org/english/tratop_e/dispu_e/cases_e/ds267_e.htm,
last consulted on April 22nd, 2006

WTO. DS309. China — Value-Added Tax on Integrated Circuits.
http://www.wto.org/english/tratop_e/dispu_e/cases_e/ds309_e.htm,
last consulted on April 22nd, 2006

WTO. n.d. Accessions: The Mandate. Relevant WTO Provisions.
http://www.wto.org/English/thewto_e/acc_e/acc7_3_e.htm,
last consulted on February 12, 2006.

WTO. n.d. The process — Stages in a typical WTO dispute settlement case.
http://www.wto.org/english/tratop_e/dispu_e/disp_settlement_cbt_e/c6s3
p1_e.htm, last consulted on April 22nd, 2006

WTO. Semi annual reports on antidumping, 2001-2003, several volumes.
http://www.wto.org/english/tratop_e/adp_e/adp_e.htm,
last consulted on December 5th, 2005

Xinhua. March 24th, 2000. China concludes talks with Poland, Kyrgyzstan. Accessible at http://www.lexisnexis.com/

Yamada, Tetsuo. 2005. Relevance and Applicability of the UNIDO Industrial Statistics Database for Research Purposes. United Nations Statistics Division ESA/STAT/AC.105/21.

Yang, Yongzheng. 1999. Completing the WTO Accession Negotiations: Issues and Challenges. The World Economy 22 (4): 513-532.

Yang, Yongzheng. 2000. China's WTO accession: why has it taken so long? Asia Pacific School of Economics and Management Working Paper. http://unpan1.un.org/intradoc/groups/public/documents/APCITY/UNPAN 002258.pdf

Yarbrough, Beth V., and Robert M. Yarbrough. 1986. Reciprocity, Bilateralism, and Economic 'Hostages': Self-Enforcing Agreements in International Trade. International Studies Quarterly 30 (1): 7-21.

Yongtu, Long. 2000. On the Question of Our Joining the World Trade Organization. The Chinese Economy 33 (1):5-52.

Danny Paau / Herbert Yee (eds.)

Return of the Dragon
US-China Relations in the 21st Century

Frankfurt am Main, Berlin, Bern, Bruxelles, New York, Oxford, Wien, 2005.
XII, 314 pp.
ISBN 978-3-631-53523-3 · pb. € 56.50*

A rising China immediately raises two pressing questions. First, the
phenomenal growth of Chinese power occurred at the same time as the
equally eye-catching display of hostile confrontations and conflicts between
China and the United States from the mid-1990s into the early 2000s. How
the lone super power of the post-Cold War world and the former Celestial
Emperor of Asia that is again on the rise will accommodate each other and
the impact that this may have are issues of grave concern to scholars. Second,
the world of the twenty-first century has changed significantly, especially in
the Asia-Pacific region. How the players in the region – who themselves have
undergone many changes – perceive and respond to the interaction between
the two titans are important questions for scholars of Sino-US relations. It is
precisely these questions that this volume seeks to shed light on. It explores
selected themes in Sino-US relations in the new century and examines how
players in the region, as individuals or as blocs, act upon or react to the
interaction between the two giants.

Contents: Sino-US relations · *China threat* perceptions · The changing balance
of power in East, Southeast, and South Asia · US China policy

Frankfurt am Main · Berlin · Bern · Bruxelles · New York · Oxford · Wien
Distribution: Verlag Peter Lang AG
Moosstr. 1, CH-2542 Pieterlen
Telefax 00 41 (0) 32 / 376 17 27

*The €-price includes German tax rate
Prices are subject to change without notice
Homepage http://www.peterlang.de

Peter Lang · Internationaler Verlag der Wissenschaften